Don't Bother To Dress Up

Don't Bother To Dress Up

A Time Filled with Tears, Laughter, Dementia and Some Very Brief Encounters

Maly Sayle

Matador
9 Priory Business Park,
Wistow Road, Kibworth Beauchamp,
Leicestershire. LE8 0RX
Tel: 0116 279 2299
Email: books@troubador.co.uk
Web: www.troubador.co.uk/matador
Twitter: @matadorbooks

ISBN 978 1838594 718

British Library Cataloguing in Publication Data.
A catalogue record for this book is available from the British Library.

Printed and bound in Great Britain by 4edge Limited
Typeset in 11pt Minion Pro by Troubador Publishing Ltd, Leicester, UK

Matador is an imprint of Troubador Publishing Ltd

For Emma, Georgie and JonJon
who were always there through the hard times.
For my sister Nicola, without whose love and support
this book would never have been completed.
Finally for Nick, my wonderful Yorkshireman.

Prologue

I'm pouring my second glass of wine. It's ten thirty in the morning. This second glass is to keep the first glass company. I look out of the kitchen window at the skip, now filled to the brim with my once precious possessions that now just look like crap to me. I'm going to have to order a second skip

I'd still be on the first glass if this bloody woman, together with her aggressive looking husband and morose teenage son, hadn't turned up YET AGAIN to see the house. They've prattled on about 'possibly' making an offer. What does that even mean? Maybe it's a hobby and they just spend weekends wandering around people's houses. I found it a little disconcerting on their first visit when she checked the contents of my fridge but now, watching her on her fourth visit, checking the contents of my fridge again, I'm past caring. Mind you, if she touches the wine I'll rip her head off.

"Is that your husband getting a ladder out of the back of his van?" I ask, leaning against the cooker, slowly sipping my wine.

"Yes. Hope you don't mind but he's going to check the roof out".

"Knock yourselves out," I say, praying he slides off and does precisely that.

Dear God. Will someone PLEASE make a bloody offer on the bloody house.

I sway my way upstairs and carry on sifting through William's shoes. I take one shoe from each pair and chuck it out of the bedroom window. Some land in the skip. Most hit the roof of fridge roof inspecting family's van. That'll be a nice surprise for them when they get home. Maybe they have a one-legged friend with a penchant for thity five year old Gucci loafers. I chuck the remaining single shoes back in the cupboard.

Next, the suits. I go at them with the electric carving knife William bought me as an anniversary present two years ago. I imagine it's him I'm slicing and not his suits. As I rip my way through pinstripe, tweed and wool I hear a yelp and catch sight of the roof inspector as he drops past the window. A satisfying thud as he lands on the ground.

I suppose I could have warned him about the loose roof tiles but I have others things on my mind.

Roof fridge checkers are now inspecting the paintwork in the house. As I make my way downstairs I hear whispered comments such as "What made them pick that colour I wonder". I look out of the window into the garden and can still make out Ed's crude painting of a naked fat man on the fence – the fence his father had told him to paint. Four coats later and I can still see it.

My unfriendly neighbours, on getting a whiff of 'family drama' had taken to trimming the hedge that divided the properties every time William and I had a row. We had a lot of those over the past week. The once seven foot tall hedge is now down to four feet in some places.

It was a particularly bad day, when I caught them, shears in hand (who buys two sets of shears?), snipping away. I had been touching up the bathroom with white paint when I spotted them. I went out, painting of naked fat bloke in plain sight on the fence. They stopped snipping. Mouths agape.

"What's your problem?" I asked, wielding the paint brush in a threatening manner and pointing at the fence. "Did we miss something off?"

I haven't seen them since.

I just need to hang onto my sanity until the house is sold. I'll store what I need for a one or two bedroom flat. Perhaps with a little balcony where I can grow some plants. Maybe even a small cottage, nothing fancy. One of those sweet two up, two downs that have been done up. Some of them have amazing kitchens I think, as I put the kettle on for a well needed cup of instant coffee.

"Ma!"

At six foot five and, if I say so myself, bloody handsome, Ed exudes a sense of ease. I mean, not many people mess with someone that size. He's a gentle giant. Still attempting to show an interest at Oxford Brookes Uni but struggling.

'In the kitchen!'

Ed appears from the side of the house. Bottle of wine in hand. Well trained.

'You look like shit.' Clearly there's more to be done on the subtlety front.

'Thanks!'

I am led into the garden where he sits us both down, hands me the wine bottle and holds out a badly rolled cigarette.

'Spliff?'

'Ed!' I say. Shock horror. Indignation. Tempted.

"Don't be ridiculous!"

Ed puts his arm round me.

'I'm a wise man and wise man say you need to chill out.'

I've never smoked a spliff in my life. I'd never taken any drugs. Ever. Would this lead me on the path of wrack and ruin? Would I end up homeless and living in a cardboard box under a bridge?

Ed lit the spliff, took a puff. Passed it to me and went in to get two glasses. I inhaled deeply. Coughed until my eyes watered. My head started spinning. I'll probably get a tumour. I'm going to die. They'll find me and say it was a drug overdose. Can't I even get stoned without it turning into a drama.

Ed seemed to read my thoughts as he returned and sat back down. 'You're not going to die."

Damn.

"How's the packing going?"

"Not much packing. A lot of throwing and slicing."

Ed nodded. Took a drag on the spliff. Held it in. Passed the joint to me.

'How's the selling going?' he says, sounding like Micky Mouse. I giggled. Took a puff.

"Fridge family came back; with a ladder. He went up on the roof."

"Maybe he just likes to get away from his wife," Ed giggled.

"He fell off! I saw him. Whoosh! Past the window."

This set us both off. We wept with laughter. We couldn't stop. I hadn't laughed that much in, I don't know how long. It felt wonderful.

I looked through the window and spotted the fridge roof checkers and, before I could engage brain, which bizarrely seemed to have shut down, I yelled at the top of my (croaky) voice "Get the fuck out of my house!" I'm not sure who was more shocked. Me, Ed or them. They took off with speed, chucking ladder in the back of their van, disappearing in a cloud of exhaust fumes.

"Ma! I have never heard you swear before!"

Again we found ourselves lying on the grass, crying with laughter.

We made feeble attempts at packing but gave up when we found a whole packet of chocolate digestives and some 'meat based' microwave meals in the freezer.

I vaguely remember Ed tucking me into bed. I felt happy. Reassured that life wasn't going to end. That I could cope. I pulled the duvet over my head.

One

SIX WEEKS EARLIER.

My old-fashioned alarm clock clangs. It's six thirty. I scramble for the little slider and switch it off. Squint at my mobile. It's six thirty on there as well. The radio alarm bellows into life with the DJ yelling that it's 'MONDAY' and apparently 'A GREAT DAY!'

Good to know.

I quickly run through the day's meetings in my head.

Ten thirty meeting with potential donor.

Twelve thirty lunch with William. I Haven't seen or spoken to him since Friday morning and why he has to work over a weekend is beyond me but I send him a quick text.

Still on for lunch?

An immediate reply

Yes. 12.30.

Blimey. An immediate reply. It usually takes William an hour to reply while he checks that I'm not a spy or someone pretending to be me in order to gather information from him. His background in 'espionage', as he insists on calling it, has left him with an almost psychotic obsession with any kind of communication. This is a source of endless amusement to me and the children. William's never 'busy' – changing a lightbulb, buying groceries – he's always 'on assignment'.

Three thirty – Events meeting with Shirley.
Four thirty – Visit venue for fundraising event.
Five o'clock – shop.
Five thirty – skip home.

I text my eldest daughter, Lucy.

How was your weekend? Ma X

I text my youngest daughter, Jenny.

How was your weekend? Ma X

I text my son, Ed.

Whose bed are you in? Ma x

They're probably still in bed. Hung over. Or bonking. Or in bed bonking with a hangover.

I get a text from my sister, Nicky. eight years younger than me and currently visiting the parental units, as she likes to call Mum and Dad.

"Just leaving. It was therapy inducing."

I reply with thumbs up and smiley emoji. She comes back with

"When are you next seeing the PU's?"

"Not sure"" I type. "Probably next weekend?"

"Can you check on Dad's teeth. I think he needs new dentures. Maybe his head's shrinking? It does that, doesn't it? When you get old? Anyway, he's slurring."

Another thumbs up.

So much to look forward to.

I leave the house with my usual blind optimism. Ever hopeful that the Battered Bitch, my ancient VW Polo, will start. I pat it on the roof.

"Morning lovely car. Did you have a good sleep?"

I get in. Turn the key. The Bitch gives a low rumble that builds to an alarming shriek. I snatch the key out.

'Bitch! How could you?'

I shove my shoes in my bag. Get my wellies on. Kick the car in passing. Leg it to the train station.

I arrive in time to squeeze my way on to an overcrowded London bound train. Within seconds the initial feeling of 'lovely and warm' changes to 'CHRIST! WILL SOMEONE OPEN A WINDOW PLEASE?' as my make-up slides off my face and my shirt sticks to my back.

I love my job and am still – at least once a day – reminded of the 'miracle' of getting it in the first place.

After over thirty years as an army wife, and now after two years in Kuwait to finish off that life, we were finally in our own house, needing more money, I'd been looking for a job for and eventually landed an interview at a women's charity in London as an Events Manager. I arrived at the interview, nervous and soaking wet from a rain shower. Any tiny amount of confidence I'd managed to summon was now literally washed away. I hadn't been interviewed for a job for over thirty years.

The interview was held in an enormous boardroom. I mumbled my way through it and, just before I left, I said

"Yes. I know that was a shocking interview. But, I'd like you to look at this." I handed over a video tape. It could have been anything. Porn. Blackmail. Me, naked, dancing.

Before they could respond I legged it out of the room.

In fact, the video was ITN News coverage of a charity run to Smolensk, Russia, that I had organised in 1989. Long before satnav, mobile phones and Google Earth. I was relying on that video tape to prove that I could 'organise' even when the odds were stacked against me.

I had the bright idea, when William was stationed in Berlin and shortly after the fall of the Berlin Wall, that I would organise a convoy of 'goods' from West Berlin to Russia. I met with a priest in Potsdam who gave me a contact at the Russian Orthodox church in Smolensk. William, surprisingly supportive, had run the idea past the powers that be and, although they too were supportive, it was stressed that any British soldiers going along would be 'on holiday'. Disappointingly The British Embassy weren't at all helpful and said that we were on our own if anything awful happened.

I was interviewed on Forces Radio and asked for help with donations. The NAAFI set up a drop off point for food and other items. Inside a large warehouse, The British community in the Garrison helped sort through items being donated. Boxes with Union Jacks on the side were soon filling up with food, medicine and clothing that started to pour in. Before long we had help from the French, American and German Garrisons. Vehicles were offered, including Russian trucks. Paperwork was sorted. But our biggest problem was fuel. How would we refuel along the way. The AA had suggested routes and mapped out petrol stations. There was no guarantee that these stations would still be there, be open or even have fuel.

As luck would have it the Russian Army contingent based in East Berlin were having a drinks reception. After a sufficient amount of vodka I cornered an (enormous) Russian General and, with the help of an interpreter, I explained what I had planned and that I might fall at the first and only hurdle. Fuel.

There followed a long pause and then he said, in perfect English

"I will guarantee your fuel. I shall allow one of my fuel trucks to accompany you, there and back."

I threw caution to the wind and hugged this bear of a man. It didn't go down well with the others but I didn't care. It was such a brilliant gesture.

ITN also got hold of the story and sent Paul Davies over with a film crew and so we all set off on a bleak December day, with fourteen vehicles : one coach carrying volunteers and the ITN team, two vans, two Land Rover Discoveries for front and back, one fuel truck and nine lorry loads of boxed items: tea, coffee, flour, sugar, vitamins, powdered milk, soap, sweets, tinned food and clothing. For the children we had boxes and boxes of crayons, drawing books and Christmas gifts from Berlin based children.

After two lengthy stand-offs, one at the border and one at a warehouse, when we didn't know if we'd either lose everything or have to turn around and take the lot back to Berlin, we finally arrived at Smolensk. We delivered food and clothing to small villages in the surrounding area. To orphanages and hospitals.

We appeared on the ITN news for a few nights in a row and caused quite a stir. On my return to Berlin I was presented with a watch by the Russian Ambassador. It's never worked but I still wear it now and then.

So, that video got me the job. And, two years after I'd been with the women's charity I was offered a job as Events Manager at St James' Hospital. From the moment I walked into the hospital I knew I had landed exactly where I wanted to be and, when offered the role, I took it.

Two

I back out of the ten thirty meeting, nodding and 'yup, yup, yupp'ing, promising to do my best to fulfil everyone's needs by magically producing donors to cover every event by teatime.

I'm going to be late for lunch with William. I wouldn't normally care but I have this tight feeling in my stomach. We never lunch. We can't even have breakfast or supper together lately. What if he's got cancer? With four months to live? How will the children react? How will I react?

I enter the restaurant – a lovely quiet Italian place I'd never been to. Maybe he wants to renew our vows. We joked about that a few months back when I'd found my wedding dress in a box under the stairs. He'd made me put it on. It was too small, of course. I could have it let out I suppose. Maybe one of the girls would want it.

I spot William at a table near the back, nursing a gin and tonic.

I gave him a quick peck on the cheek. He looks worried. Imminent death, then. I can tell. Oh God. A widow at fifty five.

We order lunch.

"So, what's up?" I say, plastering an 'everything will be fine' grin on my face.

He stares down at the table for a moment.

"I have met someone who is going to be my assistant and help with my business."

Not cancer!

"God! I thought you were going to tell me something terrible!"

"Well…" he laughs.

"Which business?" He has so many.

"The Middle East Consultancy."

"Oh, well, that's good, isn't it?"

What's so bad about a new business partner?

"She's Polish."

She? Unexpected. Polish? Unexpected.

"How did you meet her?"

"She works at a spa in St James'. I've been going there once a week for a massage."

Jesus. We can hardly pay the electricity bill and he's going to a *spa*? That does it. I'm booking myself in for a facial.

I suppose that in some ways I can be a bit slow on the uptake. I was just beginning to wonder what his business partner was doing working in a spa.

"We have been seeing each other for a few months now."

He couldn't get the words out fast enough.

"She's had trouble with her landlord and getting a visa. I knew I had to help her."

Uptake was gaining speed.

"I agreed to let her move into the studio. We've decided to make it a permanent arrangement."

Uptake has hit light speed. He's leaving me for a Polish woman who works in a massage parlour. It's not a 'studio; it's a bloody bedsit.

Uptake crashes horribly.

I could feel a ball of anger deep in my stomach, rushing up my chest, into my throat. I swallow.

William was still talking. I couldn't hear it. I just saw his ugly mouth moving. The mouth I'd kissed a million times. Then a patronising, apologetic smile. Thirty-four years of marriage. Three children. Affair. Smile everyone!

"She's my soul mate," said William, looking unrepentant and smug.

He's a fifty-nine years old, red-cheeked, bald headed man, with a paunch spilling over his belt top. Quite the catch.

A Polish masseuse.

My blank stare made him uncomfortable. If he thought I was going to wail, weep and beg he was wrong.

"I know you're in shock…" He reaches for my hand. The hands that have been on a Polish masseuse's… everything. I snatch my hand away.

"No. I'm not."

I stand up. Sling my bag over my shoulder.

"Thank you for letting me know."

I turn and leave, without a backward glance.

I wait for the green man at the traffic lights. Turning everything over and over in my head. Picking at the scab that has unexpectedly appeared smack bang in the middle of my life. I don't love him. I don't even fancy him. I'm not sure I even like him.

We'd been growing apart for some time. I knew that. Mainly because of his career. The career that had bombed, time and time again. We'd stuck together for the sake of the children.

She's moved into the bedsit! I am officially thick. Why didn't I see this?

'Studio'. Idiot. It was a rented bedsit. We were so excited when we found it. Close enough to my office to give me an hour extra in bed. six months into my job, the daily commute started to take its toll and I decided that it would be cheaper and less tiring to find a cheap bedsit that I could use from Monday to Thursday. The monthly rent would still be cheaper than my railcard and, with William traveling abroad so much, leaving me isolated and alone in Oxford, we both thought it was an ideal solution.

It was meant for me but William, being the control freak, decided to make this his 'London office' by moving in his computer, printer and endless files. I was starting to feel overwhelmed. His need to be around me the entire time was driving me mad. This wasn't an 'oh I miss you so much' attachment; this was controlling and bullying behaviour. We rowed constantly. He was always a spit away from his 'first million', but without the charm of Del Boy or Rodney. I would dutifully hand over my salary every month, leaving just enough to cover my food and travel, or so I thought.

That's why he didn't want me staying there. Nothing to do with the "I have so much paperwork to get through" excuse he'd repeatedly trotted out over the past few weeks. He was with her. Getting a one to one massage on the bed I'd bought at Ikea. Wiping him off with the towels I'd brought from home.

How do I tell the children? My parents? My work colleagues? This is so bloody…

"Are you okay?"

I snap out of my mental scab picking.

A young woman with a worried expression gently touches my arm.

"What?" I snap.

"You've been standing here for a while. Shall I help you across?"

I force a smile.

"No, thanks. I'm fine. Miles away!"

I step out into the road. The young woman hauls me back. Traffic rushes by.

"Wait for the green man!"

Christ. Not even the green man is on my side.

No one has died, I repeat, as I enter the hospital, not realising I am saying it out loud. I get some harsh looks from visitors.

Inside, I'm numb. I'm thankful that my jelly legs are on auto-pilot and doing their job; moving forwards. Left, right, left, right.

I'd left the hospital less than an hour earlier as a 'normal', middle-aged woman, with a busy life, good job, stable marriage, happy children. I still had most of those things. Now I could add 'betrayed', 'deserted'. Suddenly I was one of 'those' women. The ones that couldn't keep a husband for more than thirty five years.

I thought I knew where everything was. Where everything belonged. In its rightful place.

I thought I knew what I was doing. I thought I knew William.

I was wrong. I didn't know very much at all.

"Ma."

I jump at the sound of Lucy's voice. There she is – tall, blonde and tanned.

"Lucy! What are you doing here?"

I spot Jenny and Ed hovering in the background. Like every parent, I think they are the most beautiful beings on earth. The three of them gaze at me with worried expressions.

"Jen! Ed! Is everything all right?"

My immediate worry was for them.

"Pa told us to be here."

Did they know? Had he told them? Was I being betrayed a second, third and fourth time?

Jenny reached out, took hold of my hand and pulled me towards them. I'd been standing in front of them stock still, staring at them, mouth opening and closing like a gold fish.

I pushed myself away from them. I had to know.

"How long have you all known about it?"

They all talk at once.

"Known what?"

"Is Pa ill?"

"Are you ill?"

They didn't know. Relief flooded through me. At least I have some semblance of control although I almost lost it then and there.

I find somewhere secluded to sit. Away from prying eyes and ears. Jenny, Lucy and Ed, braced for whatever catastrophic news, hold their collective breaths.

"I'm fine. Well, not really but I'm not ill and neither is your father." A collective expulsion of breath from all three.

"What is it then? Has Pa broken the law or something?" Lucy always was skeptical of her father's financial dealings.

Despite everything I laugh at that.

"No. He is having an affair."

A stunned silence.

Ed snorts with laughter. He's right it's a ridiculous thought.

Jenny, the sensitive one, is immediately tearful.

Lucy is furious. I know she's processing everything.

Ed looks at his sisters' faces.

"Shit. Really?" Ed pales; his fists clench.

"Ed, I know what you're thinking but you have to promise not to hunt him down and punch his lights out. It wouldn't be worth the bother... much as I'd enjoy it."

I told them about the lunch, just about managing to keep myself calm.

Bizarrely it felt good, telling them everything. I felt absolved, somehow. It clearly didn't have the same effect on the children. I'd just turned their lives upside down.

"Who is she?" Jenny was keen to destroy this woman on every kind of social media. It was her way. Twitter someone to death.

"A Polish masseuse. Apparently, she's his soul mate."

"Are you getting a divorce? I know a great lawyer." Lucy, practical as ever.

I hadn't even thought through survival tactics, let alone divorce. I shrugged.

"I guess so. I expect that's what he wants." Oh, well, that's decided then.

"What an utter SHIT!" Ed was struggling to keep his temper in check.

Jenny was crying so hard she couldn't get a word out.

Lucy was plotting. I dread to think what.

Their anger and pain was all consuming and I didn't know how to fix it. There was nothing I could say or do to make things better, other than to show them I wasn't about to throw myself off a bridge.

The situation was threatening to overwhelm me: the shock of imminent divorce, the shock of seeing the children and having to explain everything to them, the seismic shift in everything that was considered solid and permanent.

I was aware of colleagues walking past. Taking in this strange and deeply personal scene. Some trilling out a high pitched, 'Hello', the subtle hesitation from others, expecting me to introduce my children to them. Instead, I blanked them and watched them move off, a little insulted. Right now – who cares?

To be honest I didn't want to have to worry about my children, either. Not just yet. At twenty, twenty four and twenty six years old they weren't exactly 'children' but to me they always would be. I knew they had each other and would gather to pick this brand new 'life scab' together. I felt like Kate Winslet on that door at the end of Titanic. It was a big door but there was no way in hell she was letting anyone else climb on. I needed to float on my door alone for a while.

I slapped my hands on my thighs.

"Right! I need to get back to my desk." I stand up. "I can't lose my job, on top of everything else and I'm desperate for a pee." I smile the biggest smile my face can manage. I almost caved when I saw the sadness and fear on their faces.

"I don't think you should be on your own." Lucy wanted me to stay with her. I knew this was coming. She's a 'circle the wagons' type of girl.

"No!" I said, a little too fiercely. "I'm going back to the house. I need some 'me' time. Honestly, I'll be fine. I promise."

They look unsure. God, even I'm unsure. But I can't show it.

"Give me a couple of days. Then you can hound me. We'll make a plan, okay?" Another big fat fake grin. Lucy doesn't fall for it but Jenny and Ed do. We have a group hug and I wave them off.

I walk calmly to the Ladies' loo. Thankfully it's empty. I lock myself in a cubicle, wrench my knickers down and slam myself down on the toilet. Nothing happens. I burst into tears. I can't even pee when I need to!

I'm so angry. How bloody dare he? How bloody, sodding, dare he decide where and when I discuss this with the children? What a spineless bastard! He'd probably convinced himself that this was a brave thing to do – break the news to me and then send me back, with my life in pieces, to face the children. Spiteful git. He *was* a shit. Plain and simple.

I punch the toilet roll holder. The loo roll flies off and rolls out under the door. Finally I start to pee.

My face, freshly washed and deprived of every speck of make-up, is now bright red as I make my way back to the office.

I think I'm pulling off the 'everything is normal' face when my wonderful, all-seeing, gay as gay can be colleague, Paul, stops me on the stairs.

'Sister, you look like shit. What's happened? Come on, spill."

Paul and I often work together at events. One particularly horrendous evening, when guests hadn't turned up and the caterer had gone missing, he offered to do his Freddie Mercury impression. I declined. He did it anyway and got a round of applause from all the staff. Paul found the caterer outside having a fag and the guests finally started to arrive.

Right now, I'm not ready to spill anything to anyone.

"Thanks, Paul! You're such a pal!"

"I aim to please."

"Honestly, I feel a bit rough. Vomity. You know?"

I know Paul has a horror of all things vomit related. He throws his hands up and backs off.

I side step concerned colleagues – Kate, the irritating press officer, Peter, the head porter. Slip past my boss, Shirley, unnoticed and finally make it into my little office. I shut the door. I feel like a fugitive.

I try to focus on my work but the adrenalin, anxiety and sheer exhaustion of the past hour begin to overwhelm me. I feel depression creeping on me. Just one hour ago. That's all. One hour. Thirty-five years and one hour.

I switch on my computer. Open a spreadsheet. Focus, Lizzie, focus. The numbers and names and venues blur. Now I do feel sick.

A quick knock and the door opens. Shirley pops her head in.

"Wowzers. Paul was right. You really do look awful."

"No, really. I'll be fine in a minute."

Shirley shakes her head.

"Go home Lizzie. You're frightening the natives."

The relief is immediately followed by total fear. I don't want to be on my own. If I stay here forever I can pretend it never happened.

"Go on. Off you go. Get some rest. Give me a call in the morning and let me know how you're doing."

I nod. I wonder if I threw my arms around her she'd decide to adopt me.

"Thanks, Shirley."

I shut down my computer and get my coat.

"Don't look so worried. You'll be back to your old self in no time!"

That almost tips me over the edge.

Three

I don't remember much about the train ride home. The carriage was almost empty. Just as well. I spent the entire journey with tears streaming down my face.

The Battered Bitch was still parked in front of the house. I'd half expected it to be gone along with everything else: my dignity, confidence, security, future. I could add home to that list.

I enter the house that no longer feels like home. Everything in it seems ridiculous and pointless. Ornaments bought in exotic locations with memories attached – pointless. Photographs of people and places – meaningless. In those few hours, everything had changed.

A text message from Jenny

"You okay?'

"Yes. Home now. Feet up. Tea, toast and crap telly!"

She'll know I'm lying but she'll get the message. Leave me alone. I switch my phone off.

I make a cup of tea. Pour it down the sink. Fill the mug up with wine from the bottle in the fridge. I take my mug of wine and the bottle with me to the living room. Switch the TV on. The comforting sound of canned laughter. An American sitcom. I top up my wine mug.

How did I get here? Maybe William's right. Maybe I could be more French. William once said he admired French men. They had mistresses. It was normal. French wives didn't mind. I'm pretty sure French wives would beg to differ. Maybe the wives have lovers. Bet William hadn't thought of that. What's the point of that? Why not just let everyone bonk everyone else without the marriage bit? Honestly, who can be bothered?

I top up my mug of wine.

Maybe I should have tried harder. Sex had dwindled but it didn't seem to be a problem for either of us. Did I miss the signs? Was he being kind? Jesus! What is wrong with me?

"Was he being kind?" NO! He was bonking someone else.

I top up my wine mug.

I don't want to grow old on my own. That's what I've been hanging on to. After the 'stay together for the sake of the kids' had progressed into 'anything's better than being old and alone'. Isn't it?

The wine bottle's almost empty. How did that happen?

The bedsit. I still can't get over the bedsit. The casual way William brushed aside every attempt I made to stay after a London event. That's what it was there for. After a late night, running an event, not having to rush for a train, getting an extra hour's sleep. Time and again I had given in and sprinted for the last train, thinking he needed to work through the night.

I stagger to the kitchen to check my phone and head back to the canned laughter programme.

I switch my phone on. A flood of text messages. I flick through but don't have the strength to answer. One message from Lucy jumps out.

"Call the bank. Close joint account."

Followed by:

"Do it now. Before you get too pissed." She's very astute is my Lucy.

I am drunk. Let's be honest, what better state to call the bank in?

It was mid-afternoon. I should be able to get someone in India.

I go through the inevitable number pushing, 'yes', 'no', 'yes' and pronounce 'Joint Account' perfectly.

The voice on the other end is flat and uninterested.

I explain, with the precision of a bomb disposal expert, that I wanted to cut the red wire. The flat voiced lady didn't get the joke, so I tell her I want to freeze the joint bank account in my and William's name.

"Can you tell me what the last transaction was on the account?"

When did I last spend any money? Lunch with William? No. I didn't pay. I walked out. Before that. Think, Lizzie, think! You sexless pissed idiot.

"Tesco! A sandwich! Two, three days ago. And crisps. And water. Five pounds something?"

"No. Sorry. That's not the last transaction."

"Can you give me a clue?"

Flat voice lady shouldn't but she's clearly as fed up with her job as I am with her. She sighs loudly through her nose.

"Travel agency?"

"Sorry, what?"

"Two hours ago? A travel agency in London? The sum of five hundred and seventy eight pounds."

"Nope."

"Followed by a cash withdrawal of four hundred pounds. Leaving a total of three hundred and sixty five pounds and forty seven pence in the account."

The little SHIT.

"But that's my money. He's taking my money. You must freeze the account. Isn't there some button you could push, or flick or delete?"

"'I understand you're upset, madam, but I'd need both signatures."

"No, look, you don't understand. I'm the only one that puts money in. My whole salary. He doesn't pay anything in. Nothing. Zero."

'There's nothing I can do without joint authorization; I'm very sorry.'

I fight to control the tears.

"Please. I'm begging you. If there's any way…"

"Sorry madam. Is there anything else I can help you with today?"

I grit my teeth.

"My husband has just run off with a Polish masseuse who is half his age. I'm on my own. He's going to take my money and spend it on her. He's going to take her on holiday. And spend my money. He will leave me with nothing. "

I heave in a gulp of air.

"I understand you're upset, madam."

"I BLOODY HATE HIM!"

Flat voice lady returns. Like an angel in India or possibly Scotland.

"Please don't swear, madam. All messages are recorded…"

"For training purposes?"

I'm not helping myself.

"I'm sorry." I say.

I really am. It's not flat voice ladies fault. It's mine. Bad choices. Bad, bad choices.

"Let me speak to my manager. I'll call you back on this number."

"Thank you." I sag with relief. Hang up the phone and go on the hunt for more wine.

Minutes later my phone rings. It's the angel of the north.

"It's all sorted, madam. He can't touch a penny. I advise you to get a solo account as quickly as possible. You can set that up on the phone now, if you like. Or perhaps tomorrow, when you're more… relaxed?"

I laugh.

"Thank you. You are amazing."

"No problem. Good luck!"

I hang up with a "Suck on that William!" The first round may have gone to him but I was fighting back and I was going to win. I was hitting him where it hurt most. In his wallet.

I sent a quick message to Lucy 'DONE'. Then switched the phone off again.

One small step for pissed woman; One giant leap for… Pissed woman starting to feel less pathetic. I was proud of myself. At least I could show Ed, Jenny and Lucy that I was not giving in.

I was down but definitely not out.

Four

I'm sitting on the toilet, drinking black tea. Everything I bought three days ago has either gone off or been consumed.

I've done nothing but cry, drink and rage. I may have thrown up. I do remember calling Shirley and saying the mysterious 'bug' had taken up residence in my gut. I can't remember what she said. She may have sacked me for all I know. Maybe it was her voicemail. I hope it was Shirley. I must check my phone.

At least I've stopped drinking. That was very easy. I've consumed every drop of anything alcoholic in the house.

I look at myself in the bathroom mirror. I've aged a year in three days. The seven signs of aging multiplied by another seven. My hair is greasy. I smell. I haven't brushed my teeth. The few stray hairs I have on my chin are long enough to detect draughts.

I hear a car pull up on the driveway. Please God, don't let it be William! I look out of the bathroom window.

It's Jenny's car. She's brought Ed and Lucy with her.

I rush out of the bathroom. Thunder down the stairs and rush out to meet them.

I have a shower as Jenny cooks us all a fry-up. I can hear their muffled voices through the floor as I dry myself. A low rumble of concern, questioning and worry. How could I do this to them? I mustn't do this again. The hiding myself away thing. It must have freaked them out. But I needed it. I can't change what's going on. I can pull myself together.

Da daaaah! I win. I clear my plate first. I didn't realise how hungry I was. The fry-up has worked its magic. I feel quite sane. Having the children with me fills me with optimism. I'm reminded I'm not on my own. That I am loved and that, whatever happens, I'll have a floor to sleep on.

The 'floor to sleep on' becomes a contentious issue as Lucy, Jenny and Ed argue amongst themselves about who has the better sofa bed or floor space.

"I have a spare room." Jenny said.

"Yes but it's full of rubbish." Ed reminds her.

Lucy pitches her 'amazing' new, (second-hand) sofa bed and the fact that she doesn't have a nine to five job. She runs her own company.

Ed holds back. He's flat sharing with two other guys. The last thing he wants is his mother staying over. That would seriously cramp his style… and he'd probably lose a few friends in the process. Or all of them.

It was agreed that I'd be on Lucy's sofa bed. I get a wobbly bottom lip. I am supposed to be looking after them. They shouldn't be worrying about me.

"I've ruined everything."

"No, you haven't, Ma." Jenny takes me firmly by the shoulders and even gives me a little shake.

"Pa has ruined everything but YOU are going to be fine."

Lucy waves my phone at me.

"We switched your phone on while you were in the shower."

Jenny quickly clears the table. She always gets busy when a conversation turns awkward. I brace myself.

"What? Did I drunk-text or something? I didn't text your father, did I?"

Lucy smirks.

"No, not quite that bad. Ready?"

I nod. Wishing I hadn't eaten so many sausages.

"You organised a new bank account. They texted you a pin for your online account.

I did?

"You ordered a skip that will be delivered this afternoon."

Did I?

"You went into the estate agents and arranged for an agent to come over and value the house. Also, this afternoon."

"And you picked this up from somewhere." Ed holds up a leaflet 'Legal Aid'.

"And this."

Jenny holds up a leaflet about STI's and how to get checked.

I look from one to the other. Mouth slightly agape. Stunned. I don't remember any of it. I don't remember getting dressed. Or leaving the house. Oh, God. Had I taken the Battered Bitch out? Idiot! What had people thought? I must have been a sight.

"And… quite a few voicemail messages."

I put my head in my hands. Oh no-o-o-o. Mobile phones are a scourge. A plague. A tool of stupidity. For stupid people.

Lucy finds the message that's excited them.

"Lizzie, it's William. Could you call the bank for me and check that my card hasn't been cancelled? Thank you. I'm on my mobile."

Lucy deletes that message. Plays the next.

"Lizzie. I left a message earlier. About my card. Have you called the bank? It's quite urgent. I'm abroad. Call me."

Delete. Play.

"Lizzie. Will you answer your bloody phone!"

Delete. Play.

"Lizzie. This is the last time I'm asking you nicely. Call the bank. I don't know what you've done… cancelled my card or something. That's very silly. They will cancel your card too. You do realise that, don't you? So, call the bank and make sure I can…"

"Oh, he ran out of time on that one." Lucy's thoroughly enjoying this.

Delete. Play.

"Lizzie. I'm calling from an Egyptian police station. Can you call… khhrrrrgghhh ssshttkkkhhhhghhhh"

"No idea what happened there. Never mind." Lucy deletes the message.

I'm shocked. I mean, I hate the man, don't get me wrong, but I don't want him imprisoned in Egypt. Or do I?

Ed, Lucy and Jenny give me a quick round of applause. I take a bow.

"One nil to you then!" I high five with Ed. Not feeling very high or five to be honest.

I take my mobile from Lucy.

"I'm going to call Shirley. Let her know I'll be back on Monday. That's assuming I haven't already been fired."

"Does she know?"

I shake my head, no.

"I'll tell her everything on Monday."

I was dreading it. I wanted to go back to work. Quite desperate to, in fact. Take my mind off all the petty little thoughts racing around my head. All the 'what ifs' and 'whys'. Take my mind off the black cloud racing towards me. I'll throw myself into work. The only bit of control I felt I had left. Get up, get dressed, go to work, come home, go to bed. Everything that happened in between all that? I couldn't see it. I couldn't imagine it. But I know I would deal with it. Step by step. Whether I wanted to or not.

Everyone had a task. "Lucy – clear all bedrooms, except mine; Jenny – go through everything in your father's study without setting fire to it. Ed – direct skip-man when he arrives. Fill said skip with contents of garage and shed. In the meantime, I shall make tea, find biscuits and clear the kitchen of pointless shite".

Just as we all started on our individual tasks the estate agent arrives. Tightly packed in a shiny blue suit and hideously pointed shoes that squeak and slide. He struts around like God's gift and makes the mistake of winking at Jenny and Lucy.

"Ladies."

Jenny and Lucy remain pan faced. They're not in the mood for flirting.

"Y'know, the last lot that lived here got divorced after a couple of years and the couple before them. Maybe we should put that in the info." The estate agent brays with laughter. Yes, divorce is such good comedy material.

"Let's start upstairs," I suggest and immediately recognise the error of my judgement.

"Aye, aye! And we're not even on first name terms!" He squeaks and slides across the kitchen floor. Christ. It was going to be a long day.

As an army child and then an army wife, I craved a home of my very own. With my own furniture. I remember watching my mum making each place as homely and individual as she could with ornaments and pictures on the walls. She'd sometimes move the furniture around while dad was out.

When Mum moved furniture around we knew it wasn't just for cleaning or for want of a change. Sometimes it was just a way of getting rid of pent up frustration. I remember one time Mum and Dad had had a punch up and Mum refused to go to a dinner in the Sergeants' Mess with Dad. So, while he was away having a 'good time', Mum moved all their bedroom furniture around. How she did this on her own? I had no idea but the bed went to the other side of the room and everything else slotted in around it. Dad eventually came home somewhat the worse for wear. We could hear him creeping up the stairs in the dark then trying to open their bedroom door without making a noise.

We waited, knowing he was now undressing in the dark. We heard a heavy sigh and then a THUD as, fully stretched out, Dad hit the floor. All we heard was "SHIT" and then silence. We didn't dare make a sound.

When William left the Army, we finally looked for a house. We didn't want anything fancy, just somewhere of our own; empty and ready to move into; near a railway station so I could commute into London. William could start his Middle East consultancy business and work from home.

We'd always liked Oxford and quickly found a house for sale, described as "A deceptively spacious four-bedroom family house with rural views, double garage, generous driveway and garden".We didn't exactly fall in love with it but it would certainly help in settling us into non Army life. Sadly it was on a main road, that ran through a 'one horse' village with no shops but not too far from the station but we were excited. We couldn't move in fast enough.

Life was then all about survival. Surviving on William's army pension and my salary. We had a huge mortgage. Thankfully we didn't have to worry too much about the children. They were kind of 'sorted' though not entirely independent. Lucy was renting a small flat, Jenny was flat sharing with a bunch of girls and Ed was floating between a flat share, Uni and occasionally coming home with his washing. I didn't see them as often as I'd have liked. I was lonely.

I tried my hardest to love this house but I hated it. Every window looked out onto a field, hedge or the main road. The garden was just grass.

So here we are, less than two years later, waiting for the 'For Sale' sign to go up outside.

Finally, shiny squeaky man is finished with his measuring and photographing and slides his way out of the house. His branded mini almost collides with the arriving skip.

"ED!"

Ed took over the skip business. I found out later he'd tipped the driver with a ten pound note he'd found on the side in the kitchen. How was he to know it was my last ten pounds.

We throw ourselves into filling the skip. Everything from the shed and garage goes in. Lucy rescues a perfectly good table lamp.

"Shouldn't we sell some of this? Car boot or something?"

That's a good point.

"Right! New pile!"

I lay an old blanket on the ground near the skip.

"Car boot blanket!"

A shriek from inside the house. Jenny.

We all rush to the study and find Jenny, with what can only be described as, the most evil look on her face. Up-lit by the light from the laptop she was staring at. I was waiting for the 'mwah ha haaaa'. But instead she turned the laptop to face me.

"Look what I found."

She's found a camera and, being cautious (OK, nosy) she plugged it in to see it what was on it.

"Who is that?" I asked.

"Who do you think?"

I take a closer look. Lucy and Ed crowd in behind me. "Oh, my God. It's her."

Jenny nodded. Lucy flicks to the next photo.

"With Pa."

And the next. And the next.

The photos have been taken at the bedsit. Gosh, they are having a good time.

Lucy takes the laptop.

"Right, Ed, go and buy a bottle or two of wine."

That's when I find out he'd tipped the skip man with my last tenner. Lucy hands over some money.

"Jen, put some paper in the printer. Let's have some fun."

I watch as Lucy prints off every single photo. This is out of my hands. I'm not even being asked if I'm OK with this. This is something they need to do. Obviously. Don't mind me.

Ed returns with the wine and we spend the next two hours drawing moustaches, spots, glasses, missing teeth on the photos. Childish? Absolutely. What I really want to do is shred, burn and stab the photos. Followed by cry, scream and maybe vomit. But looking at Lucy, Jenny and Ed crying with laughter as they try to outdo each other with marker pens... I can do all that later.

As they carry on releasing pent up rage I email my

notice to the landlord at the bedsit. Just one more month's rent payment and hopefully the deposit back. And, of course, I won't let William know.

Five

I'm not quite sure what I was thinking when I decided to have one final party before the house was sold but here I was. Sweating away over dips, tarts and salads when the first guest arrived.

'Hello? Is it me you're looking for?'

My sister, Nicky, always greeted me with the Lionel Ritchie song. She loved winding a ballad into a conversation. I responded with the usual"I can see it in yer' eeeeyes!"

"You haven't killed yourself then!" She plonks a clinking carrier bag down on the kitchen table.

"Champagne, vodka, gin, lemons and limes. For the drowning of sorrows."

She gives me a quick, solid hug. Nicky's a few – never to be mentioned out loud – years younger than me. Whereas I take after Dad, tall, fair, blue eyes, Nicky takes after Mum. Short, dark, green eyes. She was also inexplicably strong. Physically. Dad used to say it was because she was closer to the ground.

"You know I never liked William. Pompous twat."

Nicky and William only ever had a handful of conversations. She set light to his newspaper once, whilst he was reading it. He thought it was normal behavior to read at the table and Nicky thought it was just plain rude. His 'intellectual' showmanship really rubbed her up the wrong way. Now she could freely vent her dislike of him.

"I still can't believe it. Except that I can. The Polish masseuse bit. Gross!"

I nod.

"Without wishing to state the obvious, you two haven't looked happy for years." She said, stating the obvious.

"How you feeling?" She looks at me. There's genuine concern.

"I'm okay. Apart from the constant headache, feeling I'm going to be sick and want to punch someone, I'm fine!"

"Excellent. Hold on to that anger. It will get you through all sorts."

Nicky makes us both a G and T with an obscene amount of gin.

"I assume you're getting a divorce?"

Nicky always got straight to the point. I sometimes wondered if she had a bit missing. Empathy, subtlety or just basic politeness.

"I expect so. Haven't got around to it yet."

"Well don't leave it too long. You don't want to give the twat time to hide his fortune and plead poverty!"

We both laugh at that. William... fortune. If only.

"Probably be cheaper to have him knocked off. Just

saying." Nicky would happily take the job on herself. She's offered more than once.

Nicky looks me up and down. I'm in my pyjamas and in need of a shower.

"Any danger of you having a shower and, ooh, I don't know, dressing?"

A good turnout, by all accounts. I know a lot are here to find out what state the dumped lady is in. Relationship rubbernecking. Comparing my situation to whatever state their own marriage is in. There's an overwhelming air of false jollity. Like you get at a New Year's Eve party. Overly happy with an underlying sense of disappointment and dread.

I stood by the front door and greeted each guest as they arrived.

Lucy pressed a glass of G and T in my hand.

"All you need is a slipper in your mouth, and the picture would be complete. You look like a Golden Retriever waiting for its owner to come home."

"I have to mingle, don't I?"

Lucy led me, like an aged aunt, into the living room. It looked much nicer now that Ed had removed all the military crap. Seriously, how many cap badge displays did one man need?

I was kissed and squeezed and reassured.

I tried my best but it was hard. I felt embarrassed. I felt naked. Greeted with sad-eyed concern or, worse still, sympathetic smiles. No one's died. Unfortunately.

It all got too much. I sidled out of the room unnoticed. Ran upstairs and locked myself in the bathroom. Sat on the loo and sobbed. Deja vu but without me punching the toilet roll holder. My self-indulgent wallowing was interrupted.

"Everyone can hear you, y'know! If you're going to wallow can you do it quietly?"

Nicky. See what I mean about subtlety?

I splash water on my face.

"I'm fine! I'll be out in a minute."

"Bollocks you are fine. Open the door."

I open the door. Nicky has one of William's ridiculous army hats on.

"Can I burn this, please?"

"Yes. When everyone's gone. You can do all the hats."

"Okay, now I'm excited."

We retreat to the kitchen. Nicky washes up anything and everything she can find, even the glass I'm holding is snatched away and scrubbed. The kitchen sink is her 'go-to' place at any social gathering. Her back to the room. In a world of her own.

"Oh, leave that, Nicky. We can do it all later." I know she won't leave it.

"No. I'm doing it now. Anyway, if I hear one more, 'How's Lizzie *really* doing' there will be a punch up. Seriously, how about they go and talk to *you*?"

"People don't know what to say."

"Rubbish. They know exactly what to say. They just don't have the courage. So I said you were doing fine and that the heroin addiction is temporary and that I was glad you'd gone on the game to make ends meet."

I laugh.

38

"So, how did it go with Mum and Dad?" I'd asked Nicky to tell Mum and Dad what had happened. I couldn't face doing it myself.

"Oh, y'know, Dad was upset. Took him about ten minutes to get the word 'bastard' out but when he did, he did so with conviction! Mum said she'd never liked William then went on about that bloke you went out with. The one with the sports car and villa in Majorca. You should have married him."

'You know that was over thirty years ago?"

"I know. You should never have let them stay at the villa."

I look out of the kitchen window as a little blue Nissan Micra cautiously parks beside the Battered Bitch.

"Mum and Dad are here."

Nicky throws off her rubber gloves and joins me at the window.

"How long are they staying?"

"A couple of hours. I did say they could stay the night but Mum wants to get back."

Nicky nods "Small blessings."

Nicky and I wait at the front door as Mum and Dad take an age to get out of the car. Mum is wearing a coat that's at least four sizes too big, with enormous black buttons. Dad looks his usual 'friendly granddad' self in pale blue and beige.

Nicky helps Mum out of her coat as Dad, his face a picture of sadness, sympathy and pain, heads straight for me. He wraps me in a tight hug. Pats my hand to let me know how much he feels for me. I manage to hold back the tears.

"G and T Mum?" Nicky leads mum into the kitchen. "I like your coat. Is it new?"

Dad indicates that he needs a pen or pencil. I scramble around in the hall table. Find a pen and an old address book with a good number of blank pages.

Dad writes:

Sorry. Shit husband.

I nodded.

Dad writes:

"Mum mad. Angry".

I smile.

"Yep! We all know that!"

Dad writes:

"I love you".

"I love you too, Dad."

I quickly walk away otherwise I'd end up a sobbing heap on the floor. Dad follows, like a little boy, wondering if he'd done something wrong. He hadn't. I reach for his hand. Everything's all right.

A couple of years earlier, on his way from Bournemouth to London on the train, Dad had experienced the most horrendous pain in his head. He told me afterwards that it had passed after a while, and he'd carried on to meet up with friends from his army days and thought nothing of it until a few weeks later, when he realised he was starting to forget words. I noticed it too when he told me that he'd put the coffee on the cat, instead of on the table, and seemed to get really cross with himself.

A visit to the doctors and several trips to hospital for a CT scan confirmed what we all feared. He'd had a mild stroke and several since. Each one took a little more away from his speech.

This was a man whose whole life had been about speaking. Charming whomever he needed to charm to progress his army career. Make people laugh. It was a devastating blow for him. And for Mum too. Mum had never, during their entire marriage, been the centre of attention or the main decision maker. Now, with Dad's inability to speak and days of silence Mum was deeply affected too.

I desperately wished he could speak today. If anyone could have said the right thing to me, it would be Dad, with his wit and sharp sarcasm. But the drive from Bournemouth had taken it out of him. All he could do today was make tutting noises and hug me.

We join Nicky and Mum in the kitchen.

"Hello, Mum!" I hug her. She pats me on the back. There's going to be a lot of that today.

"I've bought some crisps and sausage rolls. But I'll keep them in my bag for now." Mum pats her handbag. Like she's 'packing' a gun. If she had been packing a gun she certainly would have used it today. Not necessarily on me, although she did throw a carving knife at me once, "accidentally" of course. It hit me on the forehead. I have a scar to prove it. No, today she would have used it on some poor innocent female that made the fatal error of talking to my dad.

Mum has always been tricky at social gatherings. Dad is popular, even now and despite not being able to speak, he's charming, funny and handsome. Mum has always been insecure. I don't think Dad made much effort to raise her confidence. Dad was a born performer and regularly put on pantomimes for the army wherever he was stationed. They had a great social life, as Dad climbed the ranks. But if Mum saw Dad were chatting to one of the wives she would make it clear she wasn't happy. The poor wife would be met with an icy stare and given the cold shoulder. Dad would suffer weeks of silence. Mum could win medals for sulking.

The dining table buckles under the weight of the food laid out. There'll be no more FHB (family hold back) today. Guests mill about, juggling plates and glasses. Alcohol flowed.

Everyone's a bit loud. Like the end of term at school there's a sense of devil may care. Knowing the house was on the market no one cared if they dropped food on the carpet or spilt wine over the furniture. I was half expecting someone to skip the toilet and just pee in a plant pot.

Nicky joins me in the dining room. "You know that coat Mum was wearing?"

"What about it?"

"I think she stole it."

"Don't be daft."

Nicky nods, convinced. "It's still got a price label in it."

"Maybe she forgot to take it off."

"And the plastic security thing?"

"No!"

We looked over at where Mum sat on the beaten up old chaise lounge Mum and Dad had given me twenty odd years ago, staring into space with an anxious expression on her face. She was clutching her handbag as if she were afraid someone might steal it.

"Those sausage rolls have no chance of escape. I better take her some food."

I make my way across the room and sit with Mum. Mum knocks the plate of food out of my hand. A few guests gasp, go to her aid but mum's having none of it.

"You stole this." Nicky rushes over and puts a placating hand on Mum's arm. It's shrugged off.

"This is mine. You stole it."

For a minute, I was confused. Is she talking about the coat?

Mum gets to her feet and dramatically points at the chaise lounge.

"You stole this. You came into the house while I was out and stole it."

All eyes swivel towards me.

"No, I didn't. You and Dad gave it to me. Years ago."

I notice Dad, standing like a scolded dog in the corner, waiting for Mum's anger to pass.

I'm not sure if I'm more alarmed at Mum's outburst or the looks of condemnation from the guests. Er, hello? Innocent until proven guilty, anyone?

"I didn't steal your chaise lounge. Mum, You and Dad gave it to me years ago. Remember?"

I look at Nicky for support. Nicky shakes her head, just to wind me up and mouths 'How could you!' Bitch!

"Look, if I'd wanted to steal it I would have made sure you were out, hired a van and got some burly fella to haul it out of your living room window because nothing fits through your ridiculously narrow front door." I laughed nervously, having just won the platinum shovel award for hole digging.

I turn to Mum. "Remember? You didn't have room to put it anywhere?"

Mum's eyes narrowed 'I am so disappointed in you!'

Nicky takes her by the hand "Come on Mum, let's go and have a look at the garden. Get you away from all these people." Nicky squints at me and whispers "I'm very disappointed, Lizzie." As she passes me. I pinch her on the arm. She can be such a shit stirrer at times.

I thought I'd wait till everyone left, before tidying up. I'd toyed with the idea of 'tidy as you go' but that had failed. Mainly because I kept having mini mental break downs throughout the afternoon. Hiding in the toilet, hiding in the garage, hiding in my bathroom. Nicky drags me out each time.

Gradually guests left. With a simpering smile, or a cheesy 'be strong' sentiment. Most of them had seen and heard enough to report back to those that couldn't or didn't want to make it. It had been an interesting venture for me in the sense that I found out who my 'friends' were and, more interestingly, who had favoured William.

Ed joins me, Jenny and Lucy at the front door as we wave Mum and Dad off. Our nerves on edge as Dad slowly reverses the tiny Nissan out of the driveway. Nicky, waiting patiently in her ancient Mini, ready to follow Mum and Dad for at least half the way home.

"Ma... "Ed said.

Dad nudges the back end of the Nissan out onto the main road. There's a screech of tires and blare of a horn from the articulated lorry as it whizzes past with inches to spare.

"Christ alive!" Jenny almost faints. Lucy laughs.

"Ma..."

Dad finally sets off down the main road. Nicky toots her horn as she sets off after them.

We all wave, wave, thumbs up, nod, wave until they're gone.

"Ma..."

I turn to Ed.

"What!"

"All the cutlery's gone."

"What do you mean, 'all the cutlery's gone'?"

"You know, all the good stuff."

I make my way to the kitchen and find the 'bad' cutlery in the dishwasher. The odds and ends type stuff I'd collected over the years. There's no sign of the 'good' silver cutlery. Given to William and me as a wedding present. We'd never kept it for 'best'. We used it. Every day. I loved it. It was dull and worn and somehow 'soft'.

I look at Jenny and Lucy. They shrug. Shake their heads.

Someone's stolen my bloody cutlery!

Hours later, when the house is almost back to normal, Lucy opens a bottle of wine she'd cleverly hidden. Ed, clearly disappointed at having to do so, produces another bottle that he'd hidden.

Jenny finds a corkscrew, clean glasses and piles left-over food onto a tray.

We have a 'carpet picnic'. We all sit on the floor in the living room; enjoy the wine and the left over buffet.

While everyone's distracted by a terrible singing contest on the TV, I check my phone. No word from William. He's probably being tortured for using a cancelled credit card as we speak. I check my emails and find a recent one from Dad. I read it. Sit bolt upright.

The children turn to me with a 'what now?' expression on their faces.

"It's an email from Granddad".

To: Lizzie
From: Dad
Subject: Cutlery
'Home now. Tired. Mum cutlery in bag. Sorry. Dad x"

The children find this hysterical. Oh, old people! They're such scallywags. I, on the other hand, can't work out what this is. Spite? Madness? Plain theft?

To: Dad
From: Lizzie
Subject: Cutlery
Hooray! Ask mum if she'll clean it for me. I'll come and pick up soon. Lots of love. Xxx

More waving from the front door. This time it's just me, giving the thumbs up to Jenny as she drives away with Ed, making funny faces, and Lucy singing "Jesus Wants Me For a sunbeam" at the top of her voice.

I knew the relief of finally having some peace and quiet wasn't going to last so I threw myself into packing. We'd done a lot, me and my three amigos. Ed had raided the retail park a few miles away, gathering every size of cardboard box he could lay his hands on.

He'd also picked up a box of wine. One of those sit-on-the-side with the tap hanging over the edge things. No effort required. Is that a good or bad thing? I'll find out later.

Most of the upstairs cupboards are empty. The garage is an empty concrete bunker, the shed, bigger than I remember, is cleared. The skip is nearly fully.

The postman delivers an alarming number of envelopes with windows. I make a cup of tea and take a deep breath. I don't look at the contents. I just open them.

I shuffle to the door leading to the garden and sit on the step. Have I mentioned I've started smoking again? Just the one at breakfast, lunch and tea. Possibly one after that too, depending on wine/G and T intake. I'll stop. I will. But, y'know, right now I'm doing what I want and that includes increasing my risk of heart attack and stroke.

I look at the utility envelopes first. They're all sorry to see me go. 'If you leave me now, you'll take away the biggest part of me" as Nicky would sing.

I take a drag on my cigarette and peer in the first window envelope. It's from the bank. "Dear Mrs Watkins". It's not a circular or a statement. I'm going to have to take it out and read it.

After the excitement of setting up my own bank account and securing my salary I am brought back down to earth with an asteroid size crash.

The bank reminds me that I am guarantor for all of William's loans. This is one of those 'black clouds' that I knew was heading my way. There just isn't a brolly big enough to shield me from this shit storm.

I'd signed so many documents. William telling me 'not to worry' when I asked what I was signing. And, you know, I didn't worry. I trusted him. Despite his numerous failures I'd convinced myself it was 'bad luck' that he hadn't met the right people or hit on the right idea. One day he would. I signed. Hopeful and optimistic. Trusting. Faithful. Stupid.

I peer inside another window envelope. This one is addressed to William. He's not here. I am. It's probably something I've bloody signed up for anyway. It's a credit card bill. He owes three thousand, seven hundred and eighty four pounds.

With a trembling hand, I open the next envelope, addressed to William. Another credit card bill. He owes eight thousand, two hundred and one pounds. Another ten thousand, six hundred and forty three. But these are his debts, right?

I open the last envelope, addressed to us both, and see the word 'Mortgage'. I take another drag on my cigarette and wonder if it's too early to try out the wine box.

The mortgage payments have stacked up. We owe three months-worth of payments. That's not too bad, is it? I've told them I'm selling the house. I have no idea if we'll get the asking price. The bank also kindly inform me that William has been borrowing against the mortgage. So, in effect, we now have two mortgages. Borrowing from a borrowing? I didn't even know that that was 'a thing'. Is that even legal?

I have no idea if William's business debts will be covered by the sale of the house. I have no idea what I owe now, let alone in the future. Is this when I go bankrupt? Is that what I do? Or do I go to prison? I don't know why I think I'll go to prison but that seems to happen a lot. That's fraud, isn't it? Would my salary disappear? I still have my credit card. I've kept up with payments. I can't do that for much longer. I need help. I'm going to start on that wine box.

Six

On moving day, Ed wakes me with a cup of tea.

"Morning, Ma!" I grunt with what I hope is a positive acknowledgement. The last day in this house. Last day in this bed. Last day. First day of... everything else.

Ed thunders back downstairs.

Finally an offer has been made on the house. Not from fridge/roof family, I'm pleased to say, but a couple with three kids. We quickly accepted. Even though the house has gone up in value it still won't cover the debts. Not even a quarter. Yes, that's how spectacularly deep in debt William was and, thanks to my signing everything willy-nilly, so was I.

Ed's got the breakfast on the go as I enter the kitchen. I look out of the window as the skip, containing William's shredded suits and single shoes, is taken away. Three skips worth of crap. Amazing. Hauling all that stuff around with us. Accumulating mementoes and memories for thirty five years. All wiped away with the swipe of an oily (scented, no doubt) masseuse's hand.

William had returned from Cairo with no physical signs of torture, sadly. Just dented pride. He took away a pile of old furniture, stuff he'd inherited from his father, and his collection of tin soldiers that I had 'accidentally' vomited over. They were, at the time of vomiting, laid out in some battle formation or other; Waterloo, Culloden, Tottenham Court Road rush hour. What did I know? I was literally sick to death of them.

We'd exchanged brief insults. Surprisingly most came from him; he said I was "selfish", "childish" and many other 'ishes'. I knew he was lashing out because a) I hadn't collapsed in a useless heap b) I'd trashed most of his stuff and c) I wasn't going to be there for him financially. He'd lose my salary. What was he going to live on? Scented candles? Massage oil? Maybe I was kidding myself but, as he ranted and slammed around the house, I felt a great sense of power.

We divided the furniture. I didn't want to keep much – just as well as I'd have to put it in storage until I had a place of my own.

Ed slaps down a not-too-bad fry up on the table.

"Eat, woman."

I'm not hungry but make an effort for Ed's sake.

I finish my breakfast. I was starving. I even mopped the plate with a slice of buttered white bread. I was in full survival mode.

I take a last look around the house. Checking all the empty rooms. Faint outlines of picture frames on the walls. I remember every single one. Dents in the carpet where the beds, tables, cupboards had once stood. Ghostly reminders of my old life. A week ago, I'd have thrown myself on the floor and wailed. Now, I couldn't wait to leave this place and all its reminders of my 'old' life behind.

I shut the front door. Turn the key in the lock and walk away, without a backward glance.

I join Ed in the Battered Bitch.

"You okay?" Ed asks.

I take a deep breath.

"Actually, yes I am. I'm good. Really good."

Ed pats me on the hand.

"Let's get this car on the road, then."

"Yes, well, let's see if the Bitch wants to play ball."

I turn the key in the ignition. The car starts first time. I could weep with relief. It's as if the car was as keen to get away from this depressing place as I was. I'm not assuming the next chapter will be less depressing but I am determined to move on. I've turned a corner. I've survived this bit; I can survive the next.

I search for a parking space in Lucy's road. The BB stutters in protest. It's been a long day and the car barely clears the speed bumps, it's that loaded down with my worldly possessions.

Ed spots a space "There!" He leaps out and races to the spot between two cars before a 4x4 reverses in.

I slot the BB in and, with a final creak, the car dies, with its arse stuck out in the road, blocking traffic. I turn the key in the ignition. Nothing. Not even a cough. With traffic building, horns blaring, Ed and two burly lorry drivers bounce the car into the space. I'm too embarrassed to mention that I had forgotten to put any petrol in the bloody thing. I'll sort that out when no one is looking.

Lucy comes out to meet us. "Well, the neighbours definitely know you've arrived!"

Lucy's garden flat is a perfect two-bedroom pad. Small, compact. Easy to clean, if Lucy knew the meaning of the word 'clean'. Unlike most people, she doesn't see mess or dirt. She's so focused on LIFE that the idea of cleaning or tidying just doesn't figure. Apparently there are so many more important things to be getting on with.

The spare room is just big enough for a single bed and nothing else. Lucy's allocated drawers, shelf and wardrobe space for me in her bedroom. Ed piles all my belongings on to the bed. My spirits plunge. This is it. It's all become very real. I'm no longer the parent. Lucy is. I want to kill William. I am going to kill William. Metaphorically.

Lucy pops her head round the door. "All right?"

I nod. A wobbly smile that turns into a sob. Lucy comes in and wraps her arms around me. "Aw, ma. Everything's going to be all right. Just chill out. okay?"

I sob. "I'm so sorry!"

"Shut up, woman. You've got nothing to be sorry about."

Lucy unwraps herself from me. "I've got something for you. A kind of getting-out-of-house-warming present. Come on!"

Lucy leads me out into the little garden where she unveils a bright pink bike, complete with bright pink cycle helmet and lock.

"It's second hand but the man at the shop has fixed it up. Gears, brakes and all that."

She plonks the pink helmet on my head. "Happy riding, ma!" Ed snorts with laughter.

"OH MY GOD! I haven't had a bike since you were all little!" I test ride the bike up and down the ten-foot-long garden path. I love it. I absolutely love it. Just the feeling of moving my limbs makes me feel weirdly alive.

"Can I go for a ride?" What am I, eight years old?

Lucy and Ed roll their eyes at me.

I take the bike through the flat and out of the front door and set off down the road, a little wobbly at first. Lucy waves "Don't fall off!"

Ed looks terrified for me. "Don't get lost!... or run over... shit. Is this a good idea?"

Despite the noise, the stink and the continuous near death experiences in heavy traffic, I bloody love this bike. I'm sure I won't love it when it's raining or freezing cold but right now this is one of the most liberating things I've done in years. No one knows me. I don't need to be anywhere for anyone. In fact, I don't even need to think about anyone. If I cycle every day I'll get calves. On my legs. I've never had calves. I've got Dad's legs. Long ankles, mum used to say. Once, when I was a young trendy Georgie girl (circa 1968), I bought myself the most amazing pair of white patent leather boots. The top of the boot was a good inch away from leg flesh. Dad said my legs looked like tulips in a bucket. I've never forgotten that. Dad had a way with words.

When I return to the flat Lucy gives me the ground rules.

"If we are to remain on good terms you are to do the following, without question."

I nod.

"One. There will be no moaning whatsoever. Life is for living, not to be wasted on any of that 'glass half empty' crap."

She hands me a pair of battered trainers. We have the same shoe size.

"Two. You are to wear these trainers as often as possible and, if you *do* have a wobbly moment you are to set off at pace rather round the streets or get on your bike, rather than bore anyone with whatever it is you're wobbling about."

She holds out a new ipod and earphones.

"Three. You are to listen to this uplifting track list compiled by yours truly while pacing round streets. *Not* while cycling as that is dangerous."

I scrolled through the track listing. 'I Will Survive', 'Eye Of The Tiger', 'Sisters Are Doing It For Themselves'…

"Four. You are to be present at every dragon boat training session, without fail, come rain or shite!… Usually every Monday evening."

The Sisterhood was started by Lucy a couple of years ago. It consisted of a group of impressive women, many of whom I'd already met, who raised funds for charity. Whether it was dragon boating, marathons, triathlons or swimming, they'd already raised thousands of pounds. Despite being terrified at the prospect of floating on the Thames I was honoured to be asked to be a part of it, and, on my first paddle, was given the wonderful title of 'Mothership'.

"And finally," Lucy said, "You don't need a man in your life. You need friends, work, The Sisterhood. With all that you will eventually find yourself. Okay?"

Obviously, I burst into tears. Lucy rolled her eyes and handed me the trainers and ipod.

"Off you go. Two blocks. Go on!"

I had only just started to unpack my meagre belongings when a friend of Lucy's visits. How lovely. A friend dropping by for a coffee and a gossip. And then another friend arrives. And another. One of them leaves, only to be replaced by two others and so it went on.

Lucy's friends were up to speed on William's dastardly behaviour of course and I revelled in the sisterly damning of him and men in general. I flattered myself that they'd turned up to show girl-power support. However, I discovered, as I found myself whipping up a 'quick supper for eight' that this wasn't so much dropping by as 'normal' and, on this occasion, a 'normal' pre-going-out gathering. These young women all have one thing in common; that's a lie, they have several things in common; young, attractive, sporty and sexually active. Boy, were they active. I was in awe of them. They were powerful, independent and career-minded. I want to be like them when I grow up.

I ate and drank with them, relieved to be busy and thinking of anything else other than 'now'. 'Now' being middle aged, about to get divorced, stony broke and sleeping in my daughter's spare room for the foreseeable future.

I heaved an exhausted sigh of relief when they left at ten in the evening. In my day, we left the house at seven and, if it was a good night, were back home by one. tip toeing and whispering my way back to bed. Even if it was my own place. I always worried about the neighbours.

I washed up, which turned into a full-on kitchen clean, which turned into dusting the entire flat. I held back on the vacuuming only because I couldn't find a vacuum. I put 'buy vacuum' on my mental list. NO! Reality jolted me like an electric shock. Buy vacuum with what? Buttons? There wasn't going to be any buying for a while.

I clear everything off the single bed and plonk myself down. Relieved that I'm so exhausted I won't have the energy to pick over my life scab. It only felt as if I'd been asleep for five minutes when I heard a key in the front door. Lucy was back with a bunch of girls in tow. I listen to them chat and giggle. There was no attempt at keeping it down for my sake. Why should they anyway? I hear Lucy exclaim out loud at the clean kitchen and the girls laugh their approval. I am not going back to sleep. That's certain.

I throw myself out of bed. Shrug a big jumper on and join them. I don't know how many bottles of wine later but I do eventually get to bed. I'm sure I can hear birds singing. Thank God, it's the weekend. Surely, it's not like this during the week? What if it is? I'll die of exhaustion, that's what.

Seven

I've made a list of divorce lawyers. I'd been on line and looked at all the photos. You know, the ones you find under 'The Team' or 'About Us'. The men all look remarkably similar. There are a lot of Davids and Marks. I go for female and (a lot) younger than me. I need cut-throat. I need independent. I need career driven. I need someone who can wield a metaphorical sword. Perhaps I've been influenced by Lucy's friends. I narrow it down to two and vow to ask if they can wield said metaphorical sword when I meet them.

Thankfully things have settled back to normal at work. My first week back was hellish. I could barely walk five paces without being stopped by someone offering sympathy and unwanted anecdotes. People I hardly knew gave me words of encouragement or a hug or a reason to laugh. Like the hospital Chaplain "Please don't turn into one of those bitter old bags. You won't, will you?" I promised not to. Worst though were the people I didn't know with anger issues, who felt the need to recount their own acrimonious divorce proceedings.

I went to meetings and, ninety per cent of the time I was 'present'. But sometimes my mind was elsewhere and, at one meeting, after discussing forthcoming events I said 'Thank you, everyone. Love you!" From that point on, all following emails from two of the women at the meeting were signed off with 'Love you too!'

Shirley, my boss, was very sympathetic. Compassionate leave was kindly offered and gratefully turned down. The last thing I needed was time off. I wanted work. Lots of work. As luck would have it, I had back to back events for the next couple of months.

Shirley had never liked William. Nothing new there. No one liked William, except William. He thought he was terrific. She reminded me of the last time William attended an event. He had, in his typical controlling way, tried to take over. Everything from reprimanding my colleagues for nipping out for a cigarette when all the guests were seated for dinner to handing out his business card to guests when he thought I wasn't looking. I was mortified when the next day, expecting a pat on the head for an event well done, I was told to get a grip on my husband and that he was banned from all forthcoming events.

At work I thought I spotted a few smirks from men. A husband leaving his wife of thirty five years for younger model wasn't new, but the fact that it was a Polish masseuse caused amusement among some of the less intelligent men. It was humiliating, but I held my head high and looked them straight in the eye until I was sure their penises had shrivelled. I also taped a 'No Smirking' sign on the wall behind my desk, just in case.

Eight

To: Lizzie
From: Dad
Subject: Kitten
Nicky bought Mum new kitten! Mum happy.
Love you.
Dad xxx

I call Nicky. "A kitten?"

Nicky sighs heavily through her nose. "I thought it would give her something to mother. She's constantly begging me to come down. Or asking when you're visiting. Or making Dad's life hell. I thought a kitten would give her something to focus on."

"But a kitten grows into a cat. I hate cats." I'm a dog person through and through.

"It's not for you, is it." Nicky has a point. I don't have a good feeling about this cat.

I have chosen my sword wielding solicitor. I arrived

at her office on the cusp of a migraine. It was there, in the corner of my eye, flickering like a mini psychotic disco. I had tapped my temples and taken three migraine pills to try and head it off at the pass. But, I just knew; the bastard wasn't going anywhere. I shouldn't have had those three coffees. Or that cheese sandwich.

As I waited in the reception, downing plastic cup after plastic cup of water from the cooler. I could still feel the nausea rising. I went to the Ladies and splashed water on my face. Sunglasses. That might help.

The receptionist probably took my sweaty face and trembling hands as a sign of extreme nerves, the dark glasses because I've spent hours weeping. She gently guides me to a small meeting room.

"Miss Sword will be with you shortly. Can I get you anything?"

I managed to shake my head without slipping into a coma.

Alone in the room I eyed the waste paper basket. Wondering if I could vomit quickly – get it out of the way, before Ms Sword arrived. Too late. Ms. Sword entered. I stood, shook her by the hand then I vomited in the bin. To her credit she handed me a napkin, then a glass of water and placed the bin outside the door.

"I am so sorry," I mumbled through a wad of tissue.

"I draw the line at holding back hair."

Thank God. Ms. Sword has a sense of humour.

"Migraine," I say.

Ms Sword nodded. "Would you like to rearrange?"

I shake my head.

Ms. Sword fiddles with the blinds to block out the afternoon sun and I wondered if this was the first meeting she'd ever had in the dark with a prospective client.

We sit on opposite sides of the small table. I'm closer to a fresh bin.

"I've had a quick look at all the paperwork you sent over and, I'll be blunt, there's absolutely nothing here. For you. Financially speaking."

I feel sick again. Ms. Sword ploughed on.

"You can't get something out of nothing. The debts will wipe out anything you get from the sale of the house. This isn't helped by the fact that you are paying interest only on the mortgage. Do you understand what that means?"

I shake my head. Nope.

"It means you are not paying off the mortgage. The actual debt. You're just paying off interest. You'll still owe the amount of money you borrowed for the house."

William had filed for bankruptcy five minutes after he stopped receiving the benefits of my salary. Leaving the entire debt of two hundred and fifty thousand pounds to me. A combination of credit cards and bank loans. Two hundred and fifty thousand pounds. An insurmountable amount of money.

Ms. Sword suggested, should I wish to be represented by the afore-mentioned Ms. Sword, that I arrange a meeting with a representative of said bank and William. That I should resign from the Middle East Consultancy as a Director, something that had sounded so exotic and grown up at the time. Which of course is what William had wanted me to think. I must go for half of his army pension and I should only pay back the debts on credit cards in my sole name.

"Probably best to cut up your credit cards straight away. Do you have them with you?"

My eyes swivel in a 'I'm trying to remember if I have my cards with me" way.

"I've already destroyed it. I only had one." She nods approvingly.

"It's not my job to tell you what to do with your credit cards, but, you know." I nod.

"It's fine. I'll take all the advice I can get. Especially if it's free." God, surely that's the worst thing to say to a solicitor.

Despite vomiting in her bin, revealing my utter lack of financial nous and not being able to pay an engagement fee, Ms. Sword was happy to take me on as her client.

"I know it must feel as if your world is coming to an end but trust me, I've dealt with worse. You will be granted a divorce on the grounds of adultery."

I loved it when she said that. Not that I needed confirmation, I knew William was an adulterer but just hearing her say it in the 'I'm dead inside" way she did made me feel almost normal. I leave that dark, puke smelling meeting room company, on a high. One small step for Ms. Sword, one giant leap for vomit lady.

Nine

To: Lizzie
From: Dad
Subject: Head bang
Mum fallen Friday, tripped in Park Road on 3.40pm. "Raised manhole". Her lump in her right brow, black eye, etc. Today Mum is fine but with aches in shoulder and hips. Sue £1m to Council! .
Love Dad xx

P.S. I think Sally in Corrie Street – love her boss!!!!!!!!

If I thought three skips of crap was a lot then Mum and Dad could probably stretch to five. Sixty years of accumulated ceramic, brass, porcelain, marble, crystal, wood, plastic and glass ornaments. From tiny figurines to enormous 'objet d'art'. From an Arabic prayer calling alarm clock to a sea shell encrusted trinket box. Memories of places and people.

A couple of days before I'd received the most bizarre phone call from a serious sounding man. A man not to be messed with. A man in a hurry.

"Mrs Watkins?"

I had a sudden, sick feeling in the pit of my stomach. "Yes".

"Right. Will you be in?" He sounded faintly Russian. If this was one of William's new 'business partners' they can go…

"In where?"

"Your house. For the sofa".

"What sofa?"

"Hahaha! Very funny. If I had a pound every time someone said that."

"No, seriously, what sofa? I haven't ordered a sofa"

I can hear the angry shuffling of papers in the background. "Three seater, Petersfield Road…"

"Oh! That's my parents address."

"Very nice. Look, missus, I don't care about that. I just want to deliver the sofa."

"Okay" I mumble, not knowing what I was doing wrong.

"So, are they in?"

"I don't know. Probably but my Mum's bonkers so if she tells you to go away, just ignore her and deliver the sofa. My dad is sane but can't speak very well, so get him to write down on a piece of paper whatever he's trying to say. He's also a bit deaf. So you might have to shout."

The sound of the lorry, traffic and heavy breathing.

"I bet you can't wait to get there." I say, feeling his pain.

"Can't we just lob it in the garden?" was the reply.

I emailed Dad, to let him know the sofa was on its way and I would visit the next day. I half expected a 'what sofa?' response but he emailed straight back. He'd ordered a new sofa online and hadn't bothered to tell me that I was the point of contact for the delivery.

Thankfully Mum and Dad's friendly neighbour stepped in. He even checked down the side of the old sofa before it was taken away and found a pop sock full of twenty pound notes. He handed it over to my dad while the removal men quietly seethed.

When I arrived the next morning, I dutifully bounce up and down on the new sofa. Dad is thrilled with it. Although he has 'his' chair, he likes visitors to be comfortable.

Visitors were few and far between now. Mum is antisocial and Dad has lost the will to make new friends or socialise with others. He is deeply embarrassed, convinced others see him as an 'idiot'. I ask Dad about his dentures. He gives me the thumbs up. Writes 'new' on a scrap of paper. I know he's lying.

I find Mum in the kitchen, Radio 4 is on (always a bad sign). The kitten is now a cat, staring malevolently at me from a shelf. Mum is clutching a piece of paper. The now familiar haunted look on her face.

"You have to help me report what happened!"

"Tell me everything Mum".

"I was walking along, minding my own business, when these boys on bikes came out of nowhere. Heading straight for me!"

"Oh, no!" I exclaim. Dad stands behind Mum shaking his head.

"I shouted for them to stop but they went faster and faster until they knocked me over! I've got a terrible cut on my leg" She thrusts out said leg. No sign of a cut or any injury.

Dad tries to give Mum a hug. She shrugs him off

"He doesn't care. He was talking to some tart on his phone." According to Mum, Dad is always 'out with tarts' or 'on the phone with tarts' or 'on his way to see a tart'. Bournemouth is awash with tarts.

I ask Mum to show me where the incident had taken place. We set off, Dad following, gesturing and pointing at his head the whole time, "she's mad".

We arrive at the offending bit of pavement. I wasn't expecting to see a pool of blood or tyre marks but, I don't know, I thought I might 'sense' something. After staring at the bit of pavement for a minute and wondering what to do next, I went into the nearest shop and asked if anyone had seen anything.

"Yes. Your Mum was yelling at some cyclists going past on the road and lost her balance (on the pavement) so we brought her in and gave her a cup of tea. She was quite upset."

"Did they shout at her or cycle straight at her, do you know?"

"No. She was on the pavement. They were on the road."

So, Mum had seen the cyclists ride past and an overblown drama had developed in her head.

"She also gave us these." The shop lady handed over a plastic bag full of my cutlery.

"Oh, my god!"

"Your Mum brings all sorts of stuff in. We keep it all. Give it back to your Dad. If we knew where they lived we could drop by."

Christ, no. Mum would probably attack them for being 'tarts!' I thank them for being so honest and leave them with my name and number just in case anything else happens that worries them.

I take Mum and Dad to a nearby café where they are greeted with a warm welcome. They've lived here for over ten years and used to have a good social life but when Dad started to lose his voice Mum turned everyone away. They didn't consider themselves as 'old'. They didn't have white hair!

I promise Mum I will call the council and complain as soon as I get home. I had no intention of doing so, but I sense it will calm Mum down and make life easier for Dad.

Dad is clearly focused on Mum. His face etched with worry and fear. Mum, one minute totally fine, then suddenly 'absent'. A cold trickle of fear creeps down my spine. Mum is clearly unwell. I can't put this down to her being tired.

For a while Nicky and I had hung onto the idea that Dad might get better. Hoping it would pass or, with therapy he'd get better. But we eventually faced up to the fact that he wasn't. I'm not sure I can cope with them both being unwell. Not now. Not yet. Not both.

Ten

I am sitting in the Battered Bitch, a glass of wine in my hand, staring at three hundred pounds worth of parking tickets on the passenger seat beside me. The parking tickets had finally prompted me to a) get a parking permit, and b) don't let Lucy borrow it again. The glass of wine? I was enjoying a quiet moment while Lucy finished preparations for a 'civilised' supper party. I needed a moment to myself.

Earlier that day I'd faced my biggest fear. The bank.

My personal financial crisis was an almost biblical revelation. From finding out I was guarantor to, well, everything; from the mortgage interest payment and loan against the house, to William's bankruptcy and my being responsible for one hundred and fifty thousand pounds worth of debt. William was, of course, always one step ahead. He was the instigator of every financial decision so he knew how to dodge and swerve without an ounce of remorse or shame.

I sip my wine.

I had insisted that the meeting with William and the bank man take place on neutral ground. For some reason, I sensed I'd be outnumbered. I was hoping I'd be wrong. The hospital canteen was decided as an ideal place.

Shirley told me not to do the dumb blonde routine and said she might wander through the canteen at any given moment and that if she got the slightest impression that I was 'playing dumb' she would come over and start brushing my hair.

I saw William and Daniel, the twelve-year-old bank man, sat a table in the corner, chatting and laughing like old buddies. They'd clearly met many times and had 'bonded'. Even on my own turf I was on the back foot. Two against one. Daniel wasn't actually twelve but he was incredibly young.

I looked good, even if I do say so myself. I've been cycling every day for the past three weeks and lost quite a bit of weight. I've cut back on the drinking and, thanks to Lucy and her rigorous 'no crap' diet, my skin was a lot healthier. Inside I was a bag of shite of course, but outwardly I wasn't looking too bad. This was confirmed when William noticed me crossing the canteen and *actually* double took. Honestly, I felt like dancing and giving him two fingers all at once but I held it together.

"You're looking very well, Mrs Watkins." Is the potbellied shit head really flirting with me?

"I know." I wasn't going to let William control this meeting. I focused on Daniel.

"I have taken advice and…"

"Daniel was just telling me that he left his wife for a younger woman too!" There were so many shades of wrong with William's statement that for a moment I was speechless.

Daniel was grinning like a frightened monkey.

"Is she still at school, then?" I asked.

William and Daniel thought this was terribly funny.

"I bet she had the sense to check his bank account before moving in because, let's be honest, it can't be down to his good looks, William. And, unlike you, he's probably got more than two and shitpence in his account."

I allow a moments silence while that sinks in.

Shirley walks past. Judges the situation perfectly, smiles at me and carries on her way. No hair brushing required.

Now that I had their attention I outlined what I was and, more importantly, what I wasn't willing to take responsibility for. I made it clear that I was not taking on the entire debt and would willingly to go to prison if that's what it came down to. William scoffed.

"Don't be ridiculous. You won't go to prison. This isn't fraud. It's just a debt."

"Who said I was talking about debt? Maybe I was talking about murder. Or GBH. Or kidnapping."

It was decided that I would resign as a Company Director and pay all five credit card debts that were in my name. Thanks to non payment of school and university fees and William's bad credit record, that's how many we had needed to cover our debts. Nowadays you need to hand over a kidney just to get one card. It still shocks me that I was able to obtain five. William would pay me a final settlement once the house sale had gone through and I would receive half of his army pension when I reached the age of sixty-two. Which was seven years away. Half my salary would disappear every month thanks to the IVA I had set up to consolidate all my debts. I had already found a second job as a waitress for an events company.

In the meantime I'd eat Corn Flakes, stop buying take-out coffees from the lovely Italian café opposite the hospital, no lunches or suppers out (unless it was at someone elses expense), make packed lunch for work, no special soaps or expensive shampoos, no hairdressers.

I return to Lucy's flat, excited at the prospect of an evening with young, attractive, independent men and women. As we squashed around the dinner table, I'm on a high as they laugh at my jokes, agree with my anger, tell me how strong and 'together' I am. In reality I have drunk too much, laughed too loudly and ranted about the tart my husband has run off with. Excusable behaviour amongst friends but one of the guests is a new investor in Lucy's business. He thought my passing out at the table and abruptly disappearing when I fell off my chair was very 'rock n roll' and I insisted on telling Lucy that I had, without doubt, contributed to his deciding to stick with his investment.

When all the guests have gone, Lucy gives me an almighty bollocking. She threatens to take my bike away and sends me to bed. As I lie there with the room spinning, I decide I'll pretend not to remember anything the next morning.

I'd barely nodded off before my mobile rang. I squint at the phone. Three in the morning. It's Mum.

"Hello. Mum? You all right?"

"Do you know what I'm watching?"

"No."

"A man. He's fast asleep! In a dormitory or something. Everyone's fast asleep. It's very relaxing. Sometimes you can see their eyes. Like cats' eyes on the road!"

I sit up. What fresh hell is this?

"Are you watching television?"

"Yes. There are men *and* women in the same room."

"I think that's Big Brother, Mum."

"Who?"

"Big Brother. It's a reality show. Lots of people in a house with hidden cameras. "Day four in the Big Brother…" I can't summon the energy for a northern accent.

"Mum, it's three o'clock in the morning. I have to get up in four hours"

"Where are you going?"

"Work. Where's Dad?"

"Out with some tart."

I know Dad will be upstairs, fast asleep.

"I'm going to sleep now, Mum. You should go to bed too."

"When are you coming down? Please come to see me. Please."

"I will. I'll come soon."

"When? When are you coming."

"Soon. The weekend."

"Promise?"

"Yes. I promise."

Eleven

Lucy insisted that her business was, "just another Events Company" but it wasn't. It was so much more. The business actually organised orgies. Initially I thought it might die a death, pretty much like my sex life. Something that might (excuse the pun) come and go. But it didn't, it grew; I was astounded at the number of women who wanted in on this new and innovative organisation. To be able to express themselves sexually in a safe environment. I wasn't jealous in the slightest.

I voiced my concerns. Was it legal? Would she end up in prison? Isn't it just a fancy way of getting around prostitution? She had an answer for everything. I quietly fretted. What would people say? Bottom line was that people got naked and, y'know, did the *dirty*. It was Sodom and Gomorrah all over again. Have we learnt nothing?

Now that I'd reached some semblance of balance in my life I focused on helping Lucy in any way I could. Any offers of my paying rent were rejected so I cleaned, cooked, laundered and ironed.

Lucy ran her Company from the flat. The strangest people would come and go. One evening, when I came home from work, I was greeted at the door by Batman and found two dwarves in the kitchen, making tea.

On one particular party day I reluctantly let Lucy borrow my car. I didn't have a problem with her using it to transport everything to her party but I did have a problem with the parking tickets and congestion charge fines she managed to rack up. On this occasion I let her use my car on the condition that she'd return it to its original spot. I was going away for the weekend to stay with a girlfriend and didn't fancy wandering the streets searching for it. There it was. Parked in the same spot as the day before. "God bless you Lucy!"

I opened the boot to load my case and find it's still full of champagne and boxes of crap. "Damn you Lucy. You can be so bloody annoying at times!" I unload and plonk the boxes in the flat. There was one more box left. It was very heavy, but with a bit of effort, I could yank it out. I slid it over the lip of the boot, got my hand around it and heaved. A ripping sound followed by an avalanche of sparkly wrapped after dinner mints fell out onto the road.

A lovely old guy, who lived two doors down from Lucy, stopped to help. As we both scooped the chocolates back into the boot, I suddenly realised that the 'mints' were in fact condoms. The scooping gained pace. As we got to the last few (hundred) 'mints', I told the old guy just to leave them as they would now be too dirty to eat. "Oh. Well if you don't mind, I'll take a few to eat later," he said, filling his pockets. "*You're Welcome*" and off he went with his pockets bulging. I'm a charitable person and always happy to help the aged. I tried to tell Lucy off but, as always, I got the "Shit happens" response. Yes, I guess it does.

Not long after this, when Lucy was having a lie in after a particularly successful event, I thought I'd get some ironing done. I started on the black sheets Lucy had hung around the flat. always used at the parties for the dozens of bed divans (let's not go there). Most of them had candle wax on so, relying on the age-old brown paper and warm iron, I set about lifting the wax from a sheet.

I was still working on the same sheet some time later when Lucy shuffles into the living room with cups of tea for us both.

"What are you doing?"

"What does it look like I'm doing!" Lucy sits on the sofa and picks up a magazine.

"I've never known brown paper *not* to work on candle wax."

"It's not candle wax, Ma, and brown paper certainly won't shift it." Says Lucy, without looking up from her magazine.

I throw the black sheet on the floor.

"I'm never going to iron your sheets again! EVER!"

Lucy smiles. "No one's asking you to."

I make sure there are no 'deposits' on the ironing board and continue with my own ironing.

"So, how did it go last night?"

"It was good. I had to run the bar myself though."

"Oh, no! Did the bar staff not turn up?"

"Yes. They did. But they were… waylaid. There was too much flesh on offer."

"No-o-o-o."

"Yep. Wasn't really their fault. They were very good looking and the ladies dragged them out. I need to get less attractive bar staff."

"Or gay." I suggest.

"I got them back on the bar, though. I stopped them mid-coitus. One of the guys had two girls…"

I pound the iron down furiously. Lucy puts the magazine down and gives me her full attention.

"How's it going, Ma?"

I assume she means my ironing.

"Nearly done."

"Not the ironing! You! How's it going with *you*?"

I unplug the iron.

"I don't know."

I slump on the sofa. Lucy takes my hand.

"I'm grateful for everything you do. The cooking, the cleaning… the ironing."

I laugh.

"But it's displacement therapy. Busying yourself with stuff. You're going back to how things were with Pa. Looking after everyone. Not focusing on yourself."

She has a point.

"I want to go out. Get dressed up. Make an effort. You're going to tell me I don't need a man. You're right. I don't *need* one. But I want to go…on a date. Not date someone but go out. Out, out." I'm rambling. I feel as if I've given in too early. That I've succumbed to the lure of 'the man' when I should be climbing Everest or training to be a firewoman. I worry I've failed. That I've let Lucy down.

Lucy nods. "I know. I understand that. I just don't want you plunging in and falling for some twat that will end up hurting you when you're not 'recovered' from everything you've been through."

We sit there in silence for a while.

"There is this guy…" I venture.

"I've met him dozens of times. He's funny and really nice and a huge supporter of the hospital charity and been at loads of events and he knows I'm getting divorced and said we should go out for a drink and I think I mumbled that I'd be up for… that"

"So, he knows you're vulnerable, lonely and inexperienced in the world of dating. He's going to take advantage!"

"Not necessarily! Not all men are shits! I'm going to have dinner with him."

Lucy looks at me. Suspicious. Concerned. "Coffee."

"No. Not coffee. We've already had coffees. If I suggest coffee he'll just think I want to talk about a charity event."

"So instead you'll talk about…?"

I laugh. "The same. But in candlelight?"

Lucy rolls her eyes "I still think it's too early but, if you have to. Just make sure it's nearby. And *don't* tell him where you live!"

I look at Lucy. Wide eyed.

"You've already told him, haven't you?"

I smile.

Twelve

My newfound freedom was a heady cocktail. The fact that I could go to an art gallery after work or sit in a pub with a glass of wine and a good book without having to worry about anyone other than myself was unbelievably liberating. I didn't worry about what I looked like or what strangers thought of me. I'd been retired from 'dating' for thirty five years. It was going to take a while for me to get into the swing of it.

I arrive at the busy restaurant, wearing the one outfit I own that isn't black or grey, with Lucy's list of instructions running through my head:

Don't be too keen.

Don't let him do all the talking.

Don't go on about the divorce or William or your finances or your kids.

Don't go over the top with the flirting.

If it gets too much, walk away.

I have my own list:

Smile.

Listen.

Be engaged.

Eye contact.

Run my hands seductively through my hair.

I am an independent, single woman, going out on a date on my terms.

I am crapping myself.

I've met Mike about twenty times, in various situations; meetings, black tie dinners, cafés, golf tournaments. I've seen him sober, tipsy and rip-roaring drunk. He's seen me sober and tipsy. Never drunk.

Seeing him this evening, under the new guise of 'date', is weird. I know his face but don't. He stands as I approach the table.

"Lizzie! I hardly recognise you without your uniform." I giggle like an idiot.

I mentally analyse everything he does. He holds my chair out for me. He's always done that. He's already ordered the wine. Is that controlling or has he just remembered I prefer red? I down the first glass at an alarming speed as I peruse the menu.

"This is very odd, isn't it?" he says, leaning across the table. "I feel naughty, as if I'm going out with my teacher!" Does that imply that he thinks I'm a good deal older than him?

The waiter arrives. I open my mouth to order.

"We'll have the sharing platter and then we'll both have the blackened salmon." He has the decency to look at me, eyebrows raised "That okay?" I, the independent woman with a will of my own, nod yes.

Mike tops up my fish bowl sized wine glass. "So, how's the world of 'charidee'?" That must come under 'work' surely.

"It's good, yeah. Very good." This is going to be a long, long evening. I drink the second glass of wine as if it's Ribena.

Mike smiles "Thirsty?"

I pull myself together. Lean one elbow on the table, glass in hand, put what I hope is a seductive look on my face and say "How about you? How are things… with you?"

"Me? Oh, you know, just finished the renovation on the house in France which, to be honest, has been an utter nightmare but, it's done. Which is great. I can take the girls there for summer…"

"Girls?"

"Yes, my daughters. You met them. Isobel and Daphne? Both at Cambridge."

'Course they are.

"Oh, yes. I remember. Very pretty." If you like horses. Wow. Give the guy a chance.

"Do you ski? Have I ever asked you that? I always take the girls to Chamonix…"

Half an hour later, after I'd hoovered up my share of the sharing platter that I didn't like or want and Mike had noticed me wafting my empty glass at any waiter that might be passing, he ordered another bottle of wine.

After the main course, which I also devour at a rate of knots, much to Mike's annoyance "You really should savour the nuances…" I'm past sensing nuances.

I applied my flirting techniques. I didn't get far with the seductive hand through hair thanks to the half can of hairspray I'd applied earlier. The eye contact thing was wavering due to the wine. I am listening but boy, is he boring. I don't remember him ever being this boring. Is that what they mean with 'don't let a relationship spoil a good friendship'?

I'm not sure when Mike took my hand and started rubbing my palm with his thumb "My flat's not far from here." He cooed. So is mine and I want to go there, alone. My 'independent woman' strength has disappeared, if it was ever there.

He reached across the table and slid his hand around the back of my neck, gave it a quick squeeze. "You're a very attractive woman." Is this why French restaurants have such small tables? So they can get on with the business of l'amour before they get to the pudding? The waiter fetches my coat. Mike has paid for me via the means of starter, main and desert and three bottles of wine.

"I just need to use the loo." I stumble my way to the Ladies.

Thankfully it's empty. I shut myself in a cubicle and call Lucy. "Help! I don't want to go home with him."

She rationally responds with "Well, just leave then."

"I'm too drunk."

Again, a rational response "For fuck's sake. Wait there."

"In the loo?"

"Yes! In the loo."

Back in the safety of Lucy's flat I'm put straight to bed with a pint glass of water and a scowl. I know I'll be told off in the morning and rightly so. Lucy had arrived at the restaurant and 'politely' bollocked Mike for trying to take advantage of a woman he *knew* was vulnerable. Poor man, in a way, he obviously assumed I was 'up for it'. Well he was wrong. And so was I. I wasn't ready for dating. I decide there and then to knock the drinking on the head. If not for my health then for my safety. I didn't fancy being in a situation like that with a man I didn't really know.

Thirteen

Mum's mental health had been slowly declining over the past few months. At one Monday morning meeting at the hospital a frantic young receptionist ran in "Lizzie! It's your mother. She's been involved in an accident!" The room went silent. All eyes were on me. No doubt expecting me to leap from my chair and run from the room.

"Are you absolutely *sure*? Did you speak to her or someone else?' I asked, suspicious and wary. "She has done this before. Nine times out of ten it's nothing. The one time it is *something* it's usually trivial. Not something that warrants my driving at ninety miles an hour for three hours."

The young receptionist looked at me as if I were the most uncaring, cold-hearted bitch on earth. But I wasn't. Mum had me and Nicky running to and from Bournemouth almost weekly. With poor Dad frantically emailing 'Where Mum' or "Mum gone. She's mad."

"But then again, if I it isn't trivial then I'll never forgive myself'.

I didn't realise that the whole room was concerned and the whole room wanted to know 'as soon as possible' how my mother was. I had no choice but to go. So, like a sulky teenager, I left the meeting and drove the Battered Bitch down to Bournemouth.

Dad opened the door, patted me on the back, and pointed to the living room, where Mum sat, looking frail and with the now familiar haunted expression on her face.

Here was someone who, after a heart attack some years before could no longer be bothered, or remember, to take her tablets for her angina, was stumbling through a daily fog. Her loneliness was compounded by Dad's inability to speak. Sometimes she would say that he was just pretending, that when no one was around he would speak. I knew this wasn't true and was torn between humouring Mum and hugging Dad to reassure him.

Dad would usually be sitting quietly, tapping away on his computer or reading the paper at the dining room table looking sad and lost, trying to shut out what was going on around him. I could see that depression had set in.

During her decline Mum would ask, in all seriousness if she was mad? She wanted an honest answer. "Yes, you're mad as a bag of spanners, but I still love you," (Nicky) or "No, you're just unwell," (me). Arguing the right or wrong, truth or fact with Mum could be frustrating and traumatic. Taking the easy path and play acting calmed Mum down and made everyone's life a bit easier.

I approached with care. "You all right, Mum?"

She turned to me with a look of such aggression that I feared for my own safety for a second.

"What do you want?"

"I've come to see how you are!"

"Well you've seen me. You can sod off now. I never liked you."

I could have decided not to visit. I could have stayed at work, knowing that Mum was probably quite safe but the mum I knew was slowly disappearing. Or was it the Mum I'd always known, just being more candid?

On the day I received a call from the Southampton Port Authorities, I was in the dentist's chair and was less inclined to rush to Mum's aid.

Having uncovered some "problem" or other my dentist has stabbed my gum with so much Agent Orange that I felt my eyelid droop.

My phone rings. Stops. Rings again. Then stops. I managed to express my need to see who is calling me by using my right eye to wink at the dentist.

With the disappointed sign of a torturer being told, "We have all the information we need," he steps away and passes me my handbag. I fish the phone out. Unknown number. Dentist, with spikey implement in hand, taps his foot impatiently. My phone rings. I take the call. "Hawow?"

"Is that Mrs Watkins?"

Christ's sake.

"Hes. Het me Huess. Hou've hot my hum?"

"What?"

"Have. Hou. Hot. Hy. Hum?"

Heavy sigh at the other end of the phone. He didn't expect to get the Elephant Man on the phone, that's for sure.

"This is the Southampton Port Authority. We have your mother here. She was trying to board a ship".

Blimey. Go Mum! "Huddy hell!"

Nicky and I had spent a day writing Mum's name and contact numbers in every handbag, jacket, coat and cardigan with permanent marker. We backed that up with slips of paper with contact details on too. If we could have tagged her we would have. Not an ankle bracelet but maybe some kind of 'trendy' wrist band that connects to a mobile phone. I think 'human rights' doesn't apply when you're running around a strange town in February at four in the morning trying to locate your mother who is dressed only in a nightie. I'd have killed for a tag then.

"We're holding her here until the police come and collect her. Unless you're close by?"

"Ho. Hi'm hin Hondon. Hon. Don".

"This is incredibly inconvenient for us. We really don't have the staff…"

"Hot hip hos it?" Dinghy? Dredger? Cruise ship?

An even bigger sigh from angry port man.

"She got as far as the Boarding Gate and tried to bribe the security guys with a jar of sixpences. That gave us cause for concern. It was a cruise ship. She could have ended up in the Caribbean. You're very lucky she didn't make it on board".

No, we're not. Not at all. We're NOT LUCKY. We could have rescued her from the Caribbean.

Idiot port authority security or whatever it was.

Bless her. "Hank you hor hor help".

Angry port man slams the phone down. There isn't much I could do. It would take me at least three hours to get to Southampton and by the time I got there Mum would probably be back in Bournemouth. To be honest I just didn't want to go. I knew she was safe and would get home eventually. I should have asked about Dad and whether he knew but he was probably enjoying the quiet. Either that or he's in a state of mild panic, wondering where Mum was. I'll email him.

The dentist informs me that I need 'topping up' with Agent Orange as the last shot is "probably wearing off." I remove my dribble bib and inform him that I'm desperately needed in 'Houhampton' and high tail it out of there.

From: Dad
To: Lizzie
Subject: Mum Cruise
Mum home. Love my daughter. xxx

Fourteen

"Ma, do you know anyone that can make a penis cake?"

Yes. Of course, I do. I have a whole list of phallic cake makers in my bag.

"No. Why?"

"'Cause I need one for the launch party for my new website."

"Let me have a think."

My bedroom is now more 'storage' for Lucy's Company. Lying in my single bed, squeezed between bumper boxes of condoms, fancy dress costumes and un-ironed 'waxy' sheets, I find myself worrying about who I could ask to make a penis cake. Surely just basic sponge cake. But the… moulding… is that the right word? This is bespoke and bespoke means money. Everything comes back to MONEY. Which neither I nor Lucy had.

I know ladies that bake but how do I broach the subject of male genitalia in sponge form? With icing…

and possibly some hundreds and thousands? I can't ask the ladies at the local bakery to adapt a Buzz Lightyear into a penis that stretches to infinity and beyond. I was going to have to go to my 'go to' buddies. Rebecca and Sue. I knew Rebecca and Sue baked fancy cakes. I knew Rebecca and Sue could cope with the word 'penis' and 'cake' in the same sentence. I knew Rebecca and Sue would be at the Events Calendar Meeting tomorrow. I knew I'd found my bakers.

I cornered Rebecca and Sue after the meeting when we all gathered for tea and coffee.

"What's the weirdest kind of cake you've made? Shape wise?"

After a moment of thought Rebecca declared "A dragon. That was tricky. They wanted a blow torch embedded in the cake. It melted. Terrible mess."

"But it looked great before they ignited it," insisted Sue.

"What do you think of penis'?"

Rebecca and Sue were, to be fair, confused.

"Well, in the right circumstance… I suppose it has its uses."

I could see they put this down to my new life of sexual drought. I explained, in hushed tones, that Lucy needed a penis cake and asked whether they'd be 'up for it'.

To say they are enthusiastic is an understatement. Rebecca and Sue reveal that it's been some time since either of them have laid eyes on a penis and Sue, to be sure we're reading from the same page, brings up an image of a willy right there and then on her phone.

"Like this?"

I look at the enormous appendage and nod, while shuffling them to a corner of the room away from prying eyes.

Rebecca starts to sketch on a napkin.

"What's the bollock to shaft ratio? Circumcised or not? Big or small? Flaccid or tumescent?"

I suggest further discussion should take place in a more private setting.

Sue giggles "Yes! We can get right down to the BONES of the matter! Get it?" I leave Rebecca and Sue in high colour.

I return to my desk and send Lucy a text:

Penis cake makers found.

As the date for Lucy's launch approached I received daily updates. Startlingly detailed sketches, with measurements and photos. They'd decided on a one to four ratio. The result was 24 inches of pink glory with hideous, cricket ball sized testicles, sitting proudly on either side of the main 'runway'.

Rebecca and Sue delivered the cake to the venue and ceremoniously unveiled it in the dining area.

It looked like a perverse nuclear sex sub built to service a sex craved sea monster. Strangely, the ginger pubic hair (Sue has a thing for redheads), was a kind of hairy collar at the base of the shaft, adding a Celtic air to it all and we toyed with the idea of a tartan base. In the end, we settled for a glass dish, giving it a more 'medical emergency' feel.

For some reason, it had two eyes.

"Why has it got two eyes?" I ask Sue.

"Well, my seven year old walked in while I was about to put the pee hole on the head and, thinking on my feet, I gave it two eyes. Said it was a sea snail and that the testicles were in fact shells."

Good thinking.

"Yes, she was quite happy with that. She wants one for her birthday party now."

Once Rebecca and Sue had left I discreetly licked my fingertip and rubbed out the eyes. Lucy walks in.

"All right, Ma? You enjoying yourself? Bringing back pleasant memories?"

"Very funny."

I stayed until the event was underway. I admit, I was curious to see how her 'Launch' differed from ones I organised but Lucy told me 'things' don't kick off until midnight.

As I was clearing up in the kitchen, my safety zone, listening to the background music and chatter in the main room, Lucy came in and asked me to cut the cake.

"I don't trust anyone in there with a knife."

Clutching a huge carving knife I carefully navigated my way around a half-naked lady working the floor on all fours, past the dungeon master tightening the rope on a deliriously excitable female and almost lost my footing thanks to the Masked Crusader's overuse of lubricant.

I must confess I was expecting an element of sleaze and general 'awfulness' but it was far from that. It was classy, fascinating and, dare I say, a weirdly happy environment. Safe for women. Expressions of disbelief and gratitude on the men's faces.

Oh, and the cake went down very well. See what I did there?

Lucy was so pleased with the success of my penis cake that she asked if I'd consider catering future events. Being short of money I was willing to consider anything that would earn me a little extra cash, but fully catering for a party was more complex than finding cake-makers.

Lucy's business was doing so well, almost alarmingly so, that she had started hiring weekend venues outside of London. To make it worthwhile for guests, they needed to be fed properly with canapes on arrival, followed by a three course dinner and a simple buffet breakfast in the morning, should any of them have stopped shagging long enough to want to eat food, and not each other.

These venues, usually big country houses, didn't come complete with caterer and hiring in would be ridiculously expensive. I tentatively agreed, subject to Nicky agreeing to work with me.

"Catering for young fit people walking around in the nude? What's not to like?" she responded. "Hang on... We don't have to be naked, do we? My saggy boobs would be enough to put anyone off a skewered prawn." Clearly less concerned than me then.

We eventually agreed, on the understanding that Lucy respected our list of ground rules. If she did that then all would be well.

Fifteen

To: Lizzie
From: Dad
Subject: Mum on coach. She mad.

I don't know how Mum manages it. She has no money whatsoever. Yes, there is money in her account but she doesn't have the wherewithal to use a cash machine or a credit card let alone remember a pin number. Mum has regressed to shillings and farthings and she carries both around with her.

She arrives at Victoria Coach Station, deposited by a bus driver visibly relieved to be rid of this mad old bat. Fortunately, Nicky got there early enough to meet Mum off the bus and take her to lunch at what used to be the Army and Navy store in Victoria, one of Mum's favourite places.

Nicky would sometimes take Mum on the tube, all the way round the circle line, for old-time's sake. Mum's memories of London during the war were crystal clear and she'd revert to her Cockney routes, chatting to anyone and everyone. She absolutely loved the underground.

She was also a prolific thief, picking up other people's shopping bags. We'd usually get the bags back to their rightful owner but sometimes we didn't notice until it was too late and despite retracing our steps we couldn't find the owners. Charity shops did quite well out of Mum's London visits.

Then she'd be coaxed back on a coach home with Dad waiting for her at the other end. She was happy to go home to the cat. However, as things got worse with her mental health, we'd get on the coach too. It was the only way to make sure she got home. It was exhausting.

I had managed to arrange a visit from the social worker. A lovely woman called Carol. Experienced, kind, gentle. I spent the night at Mum and Dad's. Fighting for pillow space with the malevolent, fur shedding cat. The cat was now Mum's reason for living, it seemed. Dad had been replaced by this evil four-legged she devil. The smell in the house was almost intolerable thanks to the saucers of freshly boiled cod left in every room.

Mum senses something's up when she finds me clearing away the saucers.

"Don't do that! She'll be hungry."

"How about we leave one in the kitchen and one in the spare room upstairs, Mum. Then she's got a dish on each floor."

Then later, when I was vacuuming.

"Don't do that! She doesn't like the noise!"

Carol arrives, smiley, reassuring. Immediately branded a tart by Mum when Dad shakes her by the hand.

I make tea and put biscuits on a plate to make it feel more like a special occasion for Mum, while Carol, sitting on the new sofa, tries to communicate with her.

"How are you, Mrs. Roberts?"

"Mind yer own bleedin' business."

Mum's in full East End mode today

Carol ploughs on, used to this kind of behaviour. It's reassuring to see a stranger at ease with Mum's anger.

Tea drunk and biscuits eaten, Carol shuffles her (rather large) bottom to the edge of the sofa.

"Shut your legs! You're frightening the cat."

I just about manage not to exhale tea through my nose as Dad quickly helps Carol up off the sofa and out of the door.

"MUM!"

Mum looks at me, all innocence "What?"

She starts laughing. I start laughing. It's one of the few times I've ever cried with laughter with Mum.

It was a good day. But also, the worst.

Carol's parting comment was that she thought Mum had Vascular Dementia and we needed to get her assessed properly, as quickly as possible.

Getting Mum to see a GP was incredibly tricky as she didn't think she needed to waste his time. "I'm not sick" was her excuse. On several occasions we had to pretend that everyone in town was being checked and they'd come looking for her if we didn't turn up.

These visits were very stressful but at times really funny.

With one specialist, Mum was asked if she knew what month it was to which she replied "October, derrr". She looks at me, rolls her eyes and points to her head, making a "She's mad" sign. (It was March).

"Okay. So, Mrs Roberts. Do you know the name of the Prime Minister?"

"Yes thanks."

The *"I'm going to give you three words to remember and then get you to tell me the words in about five minutes' time"* brought on the question "Why? Can't you remember for yourself?" Followed by another bout of tutting and pointing to head. "I've got enough to do without having to remember your words as well."

Part of me wanted to laugh my head off but generally I found this very fraught as I was so bloody tired and so, so worried about her. Within seconds I had forgotten one of the words. Not that I mentioned this. One demented female at a time was my only thought.

Following countless home visits, assessments, discussions and form filling, the inevitable, and my worst fears were confirmed; Mum did have Vascular Dementia.

Sixteen

Yet more ground rules:

1. No one comes into the kitchen except Company staff.
2. No one to know that we are related (which is ridiculous as we look alike).
3. Special dietary requirements and/or extra numbers must be flagged up well in advance. If not they go hungry.
4. Any naked waiters do not count as 'staff' so may not enter the kitchen. We don't care how good looking or well endowed they are. I had to pull rank on Nicky here. She tried the 'but what if something's really heavy' angle. Fail.
5. Make sure the main entrance is clearly marked so that no one comes around the back of the building and through the kitchen.
6. We must have accommodation away from the premises so that we get a good night's sleep before returning to clear up and lay out breakfast.

Nicky is brilliant at preparing and tidying as we go; washing up is her favourite hobby. I'm good at cooking and forward planning. I'd arranged for the fresh food to be delivered before we arrived so, when we set out in the Battered Bitch with our overnight bags and a tool box full of preferred kitchen utensils, we were excited and terrified in equal measure. What the hell were we doing?

"What if someone propositions us?" asks Nicky.

"We decline, obviously."

"Do we, though? What if they get upset?"

"They won't."

"Huh."

So here we both were. Two hours later. In jeans, white shirt and matching stripy pinnies, looking very professional and raring to go. As we arrived at a huge country house, with sweeping drive, beautiful lawns and manicured gardens we felt calm and confident. We knew we could pull this off and have fun in the process.

Hours later, after numerous cups of tea and occasional sip of wine we were rocking along. Things were boiling, roasting, cooling, freezing. We took a break, a moment of rare quiet. Except it suddenly wasn't.

I'm holding a wet lettuce in my hand and Nicky's clutching a carrot, when we become aware of the strangest noise coming from above.

"What the hell is that? Is someone crying?" Nicky and I listen. I mean, properly listen.

"Sounds like someone's sobbing. Should we get Lucy?"

I send Lucy a text.

THERE'S A WOMAN CRYING UPSTAIRS!

Lucy replies.

"Tantric sex. Don't worry."

Don't worry? Don't worry? How can we grate and grind with that racket going on?

"It's just rude. No one makes that much noise. It's fake. I should know. She sounds like me. I'm going up there!" Nicky's half out of the kitchen before I stop her.

"No!"

Instead we laugh, really loudly, which leads to us really laughing at the absurdity of it. Mind you, it did shut the dramatic tantric female down.

I was annoyed that someone hadn't thought this through and the two old trouts in the kitchen were having to listen to this. Well it wasn't the end of the world – but it felt like it when an oily middle aged guy sauntered into the kitchen and asked if he could borrow the olive oil as he'd forgotten his massage oil. For a second I thought Nicky was going to retch, but she didn't. She handed him the (cheap) oil.

"I want that back and I don't want to see a single pubic hair stuck on it, okay?"

I sensed an underlying anger building up in the two chefs.

The bottle was returned, pube free, and given a good clean by Nicky.

We'd catered to the last lettuce leaf for the guests so it was a shock when five men sauntered into the kitchen, dressed like car mechanics and demanded something to eat.

"Are you guests?" asked Nicky, pissed off that they were there a good three hours before kick-off.

"No, we're setting up the torture dungeon".

"There's a garage down the road. Why not get yourselves some sandwiches?" said Nicky, holding a pair of tongs in a threatening manner.

I send Lucy a text.

"Do we have to feed the torture guys?"

"Yes, please," she replied. Blasé. Laid back. Really annoying.

Feeding the torture troupe seriously put a dent in our supplies and I started to worry about portion sizes.

It wasn't even tea time and we were knackered. Not from the comings and goings of people asking to be fed but from standing up for hours on end in a boiling hot, badly laid out kitchen.

By the time glamorous scantily clad guests arrived we looked like a couple of menopausal biddies in full hot-flush insanity. With hair stuck to the back of our necks, our once white shirts greasy and stained, with a feeling of 'fight or flight' wafting over me.

We had reached the witching hour. This had nothing to do with time. This was the point in the evening when we were both so completely knackered we turned into witches. We'd fed and watered fifty guests from a tiny, ill equipped kitchen that had open access to all and sundry.

We'd endured countless 'Is this the way to the party?' Answer: "No! Go round the bloody front!" And "Do you have a needle and thread? I've split my dress." Answer: (Thinks) "No. Lose some weight." (says) "No. Sorry dear. "We're just staff!". And "Hiya babes. Do you have any rose water and mint?" Answer: Where do you think you are? The bloody Ritz – babe!" and "I'm sensing anger issues here. Have you both thought about hypno…" Answer: "GET OUT!"

I overheard a guest chatting to Lucy "Wow, your two chefs are really angry!"

We weren't angry. We were just… okay, we were angry but we were also busy and having to work with what we had.

However, the returning, satisfyingly empty plates and whispers of appreciation passed on to us from Lucy's staff made it all worthwhile.

The washing up was almost done (thank you knackered dishwasher), gin and tonics were in sight and then…

'We've got a late one!'

Nicky and I looked out from a cloud of steam as Lucy, fragrant and beautiful in her scarlet scrap of fabric called a dress, glided into the kitchen.

"Mega-wealthy client. Broke down on the way. About ten minutes away and really hungry."

"Can't be that wealthy if his car broke down. Where's his helicopter?" hissed Nicky over the washing up bowl.

She looked out of the open kitchen window and there stood an extremely famous, handsome and apologetic man. He insisted a sandwich would be fine. He didn't want to be a bother.

"No," breathed Nicky, suddenly going all Meryl Streep on me, "We wouldn't hear of it. Don't you worry. You just concentrate on getting those tyre marks out of your suit jacket."

I went into panic mode. We could scrape together a good starter and main but we were completely buggered on the pudding. Second helpings of the ever-popular Eton Mess left us with a bowl of double cream, some sad looking strawberries and nothing else. We'd run out of meringues. I was literally on the verge of a nervous breakdown. I wanted to cry. All our planning sent to pot because some rich twat had broken down. Well, that's how I saw it. My sister, on the other hand, didn't.

'You will NOT have a breakdown over a fucking meringue!'

She grabbed a packet of Oreo's from the fridge, crushed them up and stirred them in the bowl of snowy white double cream. She then added the strawberries to this shit brown mixture.

"There! Eton Noir. If he doesn't like that he's an idiot. Eat your heart out Nigella!" Incredible woman!

I nearly died. But the bowl came back empty. He loved it. I should patent that recipe.

Lucy thanked us as she saw us off in a taxi to a local B&B.

"Thanks dream team. Everyone thought the food was great. A couple of the guests want to know if we're always going to use The Angry Chefs and whether you'd consider using a whip?"

Exhausted, deaf from all the constant chatter, crippled after being on our feet for eight hours, we said we'd think about it.

At our B&B we slept the sleep of the dead, only waking up at the sound of a car backfiring.

Seventeen

A few days later, I was woken by my mobile. I don't pick it up straight away, as I usually would. I looked at the clock. Five thirty. For a split second I quietly hoped it would be 'bad' news.

"Your mother has died peacefully in her sleep, surrounded by an enormous amount of cash. At least twenty thousand pounds which we will keep safe for you and only you".

The phone stopped ringing. A wave of guilt hits me. Oh God. What if it really was bad news? What if it was Mum? Stuck somewhere, desperate for help? I dial 1471. Yep. Mum and Dad's home number. I'm evil. I should ring back but it's now five forty five. I could get another hour and a bit sleep. I'm too awake. I'll call back. In a minute.

The phone rings.

"Hello?"

"Hello. Is that Mrs Watkins?"

I KNEW IT. She's gone and bloody died on me.

"Yes. Who is this? Are my Mum and Dad all right?"

Vision of Mum and or Dad setting light to the house after confusing coffee table for campfire.

"Yes. They're both fine. My name is John. I'm the manager of the Co-op on the high street. I found your mother wandering round the back of the shop, when we were taking a delivery. She was in her nightie and quite distressed."

"Oh my God! I'm so sorry. We always make sure there's enough food in the house but she must have felt like shopping. Thank you for bringing her…"

"She was looking for her babies? She said she had seven and had lost all of them."

I felt like I'd been kicked in the stomach. I wanted to cry. I wanted to throw up. I wanted to shout at the unfairness of it all.

"We had to call the police. They're here. We're waiting for Social Services. One of the policemen wants to talk to you".

Dear God.

In fairness, once I had explained that Mum was waiting to being assessed by the Mental Health people and Dad was sort of okay but couldn't communicate verbally, the police were very supportive and kind to both Mum and Dad. During the call I could hear Mum banging on in the background trying to convince them that Dad was not her husband but 'the man robbing her house'. The police assured me that they would put them both on their 'at risk' register and look out for them.

Eighteen

So here we were. After several more meetings with the GP and a psychiatric specialist, we were waiting for a place to become available in a psychiatric unit. She would be assessed and kept in this unit for as long as it took us to find somewhere permanent. Waiting could take up to six weeks and until then Mum would have to carry on living at home with Dad.

Any medication prescribed to Mum gets hidden down the side of the chair, thrown away or fed to the cat. Why should she take tablets? Nothing hurts, she didn't have a temperature, nothing needed curing. It was impossible to explain the word 'preventative'. Dad's emails have not only increased in number but are also making less sense. I was never sure where Mum was or had been. The calls from kind strangers were replaced with calls from the police as Mum became more difficult, physically and verbally. Phoning Dad was out of the question of course. I could hear him breathing and cooing, like a pigeon, which made everything that much more upsetting and frustrating.

Between waiting and placing Mum, we needed to focus our minds on selling their house, buying a flat for Dad and a care home for Mum – near each other and definitely nearer to us. We landed on Kingston as Nicky lived there and worked from home plus I could get there from work in under thirty minutes.

I am told that it helps if a family member is present when a psychiatric nurse arrives at the house; to get Mum out of the house, into a stranger's car and through the door of the psychiatric unit. The wheels were set in motion and I would worry about the removal of Mum from house to unit as and when it happened. In the meantime, I'm to, 'carry on as normal'.

Well, 'normal' didn't exist anymore. Dad sank deeper into depression, the cat carried on eating and I carried on losing weight and sanity. Mum, completely unaware of what was going on, carried on travelling. It was as though she knew the clock was ticking and her travels were no longer once or twice a week but daily.

On one of these days she travelled from Bournemouth Coach Station to Victoria Coach Station with her jar of sixpences, happy in her own little world. She then sat in the coach station waiting for her 'Mum' to pick her up. This time a very understanding Frenchman, who recognised the signs of dementia, thanks to his own mother suffering the same, sat with her. He found the contact numbers in Mum's bag, called me and said he would not leave her side until she was rescued. As neither I nor Nicky could get to the station he kindly put her in a black cab with specific instructions to the driver to get Mum to my office. I was waiting for the cab and could have done without the driver saying, "Get out of my cab you daft old woman" but she had sent him mad with her constant wittering and attempts to pay with her jar of sixpences. A twenty pound note shut him up.

On another day, I visited, to find Mum and some other woman of similar age yelling at each other in the street. As I park and leap out of the battered bitch – well climb out as my back was killing me – I see Mum, with a cat in her arms heading for her front door at speed. I just manage to get inside behind her before she slams the door shut, in the face of the other screeching woman.

"You're bloody mad! Give me back my cat or I'll call the police" said screeching woman.

I look at Mum and then the cat in her arms. The cat is staring at me, eyes the size of saucers, with a sort of "Please help me" look on its face.

"What's going on Mum?"

"That stupid mare thinks I've stolen her cat but I know it's my cat."

I stare from Mum, to Dad, to the cat in her arms and then to the cat lying on the sofa. *Her* cat lying on the sofa.

"Mum. You've got the wrong cat. Look on the sofa"

I say this as I open the front door and ask the woman to kindly step away from the door and we'll let the cat out. No ransom. No fuss. Just step away from the door.

Not convinced, Mum clings to the cat which, now looking at the open door, sees its chance to escape and, with one bound shoots out of her clutches and out of the front door but NOT before Mum lunges at the door to slam it shut, still not convinced she's giving up the right cat. The door shuts with an almighty bang.

In the silence that follows, I think all is well. We can get the kettle on and take stock and then the woman outside starts yelling again.

"You vicious woman! Don't you ever touch my cat again."

Before I decide how to respond, we glance down at the floor and see that half a cat's tail is lying on the mat. Mum sees the (half) tail and starts to sob.

"Oh no! I've chopped off his tail!"

"No you haven't Mum. It will grow back again"

"Promise?"

"Absolutely. It'll take about a week then he'll be right as rain"

She seems to accept this. Dad rolls his eyes and we head into the kitchen.

"Let's just put the kettle on shall we chaps?

Nineteen

It did indeed take six weeks before a place was found for Mum. I was at my desk when I got the call from a psychiatric nurse telling me that she was picking Mum up that afternoon.

"I expect your dad will want to come along. Help your mum settle in" she said.

"ARE YOU MAD? NO!"

A stunned silence from the nurse.

"Sorry but Dad can't speak. He won't be able to cope with any of it. I can't allow you to take Mum with just Dad there. I have to be there myself. PLEASE!"

We were in a Catch 22 situation. We had to get Mum to the unit today or we'd lose the bed. The lovely nurse agrees that they will wait until seven o'clock but it will be a male colleague waiting and not her as she would not be on duty. We had until seven o'clock to get Mum into that bed. It's three o'clock. Four hours.

I call Lucy. It goes to voicemail. I call Ed. It goes to

voicemail. I call Jenny, she answers. It's all I can do not to weep with relief.

"Where are you?"

"Oh, and good afternoon to you too!" Of course. Jenny isn't aware of my high level of panic.

"Sorry! But I need to get to Nanny and Granddad's. Can you get the BB to the hospital in the next half hour?"

I give Jenny the bare bones of what's happening. Thankfully she's in London.

"But I don't have the car key!"

"The cars not locked. The key's in the glove box." There's no point in locking the car. If anyone wants to steal it they're welcome.

Once Jenny had stopped telling me off for not locking the car she says she's 'on it'

I log off my computer, gather my belongings and rush to Shirley's office. Knock. Enter without waiting for her to respond. Explain, at a hundred miles an hour. Get the nod.

The wait on the hospital steps feels like an eternity. Jenny must have run every red light to get here in under twenty minutes. The BB screeches to a halt. Jenny leaps out, gives me a quick hug. I'm sure I burn rubber as I speed off along The Fulham Road.

I've only been driving for five minutes before 'poof' – flat tyre. I can't believe it. I toy with the idea of driving on with a flat but, knowing I have a three hour drive on the motorway I scotch that idea. I call Jenny, praying she's not on the tube. She isn't.

"Jenny! I've got a flat tyre!"

"Where are you?"

I tell her where I am and thank God that she's the sporty type as literally five minutes later she's jogging towards me.

We push the car into a side street. I don't care if I get a ticket or if the car is towed away or blown up. I must get to Bournemouth. I flag down a black cab. Yes, a black cab.

"Bournemouth, please!"

"Eh?"

"Yep! Bournemouth. Please don't break down or say your shift ends in a minute or that you don't go that far south of the river. I have to get to my Mum!" The tears helped.

I look out of the back window of the cab as it speeds away and wave to Jenny, suddenly remembering that I'd left my bag in the BB. I have no cash on me. Not even my trusty cash card. I decide to cross that bridge... much later.

Five forty five. The psychiatric nurse is waiting patiently in her car as the black cab pulls up in front of the house. I have by then, of course, given the cab driver the entire story. In turn, he's given me his story too. His grandmother has dementia. He waives the fee and turns down the suggestion of my paying once I get home. Instead he said I should donate to a dementia charity. All these knights in various suits of shining armour were slowly reviving my faith in men. Only joking. One prince doth not a kingdom make... or thumthing like that.

Walking into the sitting room I could see that Mum has shredded every piece of paper she could find and has scattered it all over the house. Her hair is matted, her dressing gown is filthy and the place stinks of stale cat food and pee. There are packing boxes in the hall. Piles of books block the back door. It is frightening how everything has gone so rapidly downhill since I visited just a few days before.

I find Dad in the dining room looking completely bereft and broken. Even thinner, he is hunched over his trusty computer playing patience. I want to break down and sob but do my best to explain to him what's happening and that I will be back once Mum is settled. I write down what I have just said in his notebook so that he can go over it and then call Mum and Dad's very understanding neighbour, asking if he could sit with Dad for a bit.

"Are we going on a journey?" Mum asks, like an excited little girl, when I tell her we're going for a drive in a friend's car. It's all I can do to nod and smile. It was heart breaking.

Mum refuses to wash or change, so, still in her dressing gown and slippers we climb into the back of this stranger's car. Mum chats excitedly as we set off and, feeling sick to my stomach, we are waved through the gates of the secure unit.

My tiny five foot tall mother. Someone who used to be so strong and independent, with no idea what was ahead and who certainly did not deserve to spend the rest of her life in a complete fog, frightened and confused, having strangers take care of her when all she wanted was her family around her. So bloody unfair. So fucking unfair. When we arrive I am thankful it is dark and she cannot read any of the signs directing us to the main reception.

As we are shown into a large communal area and the door is locked behind us, we hear screaming and crying; patients fighting their own demons. It was now around eight o'clock. It took us longer to get Mum out of the house but the psychiatric hospital knew she was on her way so at least I knew the bed was still there.

The nurse asks us to wait in the main lounge while the paperwork is sorted. Mum looks around her, at the television, the chairs, the people wandering around.

"I'm not well, am I?" She turns to look at me. One of those alarming moments of clarity. She needs an honest answer.

"No, you're not well Mum, but you won't be here for long."

"You won't leave me, will you?"

"No. I won't leave you."

We cuddle up and hold hands, watching the antics of other patients occasionally wincing when someone gets a little too near us. An elderly man picks a fight with his shadow. A woman scolds a baby doll she holds in her arms. The sudden shouts from patients out of sight is unsettling and frightening. Staff calmly go about their business of putting patients to bed; cajoling and jollying them along.

By nine o'clock the paperwork is finished and the feeling of 'madness' is less evident as sleep time settles in for all the patients and a near quiet descends.

Introductions are made to various members of staff then Mum is given medication that I am told is strong enough to knock a horse out. They don't know my mother.

We are shown into a four-bed room. The other three beds are empty. I wonder what happened to those three patients. I thought the wait for a bed took for ever.

"We always keep some beds empty for emergency referrals," said the nurse, seeming to read my thoughts.

Great. So, Mum could be sharing a room with an axe wielding murderer.

"Don't worry. Seriously violent patients aren't sent here." Yes. She's a psychiatric psychic nurse.

Mum agrees to stay in bed if I stay too, so I sit quietly in a chair beside her bed, like a parent trying to get a fractious child off to sleep. I try not to engage in conversation or laugh at her imitation of a vampire rising from a coffin (but, under the circumstances, it is very funny). After another hour of chatting and clowning around, the drugs finally kick in. Mum drifts off into a drug induced sleep. Having promised not to leave her I did just that, knowing she would wake the next day afraid, not remembering where she is or why she is there. I know she'll fight to get out. I know it's going to be hell. I feel I am letting her down. That I should stay and be there when she wakes up. I know it would make little difference to her. But the guilt is enormous.

As I wait patiently to be released through the coded doors, with voice cracking, I asked that they "Please look after my Mum" and, once outside, having been asked to wait while they organise a ride home for me, I find a wall to sit on and sob as the gut wrenching sadness, fear and anger surface. I have a sudden and unexpected sense of mourning. The mother I have known my whole life is dying the slowest death imaginable. I am overcome with childish impulse; I stamp my feet and carry on sobbing uncontrollably.

I don't remember much of the journey back to Dad's, other than being driven by a member of staff who lived near them and was fortunately at the end of her shift. I vaguely remember her reassuring me that Mum would be taken care of but have no memory of my response or saying goodbye to her. When I walked back into the house Dad is still sitting in the dining room. He'd obviously sent the neighbour home and played patience on his computer until I returned. He silently pats me on the back while I make myself a cup of tea. I hold back the tears until after Dad is in bed, then I call Nicky, Jenny, Ed and Lucy to update them.

I then do something that perks me up. I remove all the tuna and cod filled dishes from everywhere in the house; the stairs, the bathroom, spare bedroom, sitting room. I throw away the dishes where the food has solidified. I shut the fat cat in the kitchen with a dish of dried food. I strip the bed in the guest room and replace with clean, cat hair free linen. It's a whole new start for everyone that night, including the cat.

Nicky arrives the next day and after a hug and a weep we start cleaning the house and give Dad some much needed love, attention and freshly cooked meals. We find over three hundred pounds hidden in various places; not to mention CDs, letters, remote controls, car keys, tinned food and dozens of notes written in Mum's lovely handwriting; 'Help me' was the main theme, but also lists of names and numbers that don't make any sense and notes begging for someone to look after her children.

Seeing that Mum has been writing out her nightmares on paper is deeply upsetting. Drinking endless cups of tea we get through the day and Dad cheers up hugely. I wrote down what had happened the night before so that yet again he could go over it in his own time and explained that we are asked not to visit for the first week so that they can settle Mum in.

We make a conscious decision not to tell him the name of the hospital as we know he would try and find it and visit on his own. Visiting might help in some ways but leaving on his own would be a nightmare for him. A week just looking after himself (and occasionally the cat) will also be beneficial.

We talked to Dad about selling the house and moving him somewhere closer to me and Nicky and, hopefully, near Mum's future care home. He worries that we'll find somewhere for him and not Mum. That she'll be left behind and he won't be able to see her. We explain, over and over, that we won't let that happen. We finally get the thumbs up and a note saying "Yes to move."

A week later I take Dad to visit Mum at the secure unit and it is harrowing. Looking around, he literally howls with despair. When we find Mum, pottering in the garden, they cling to each other like abandoned children, with Mum sobbing and begging to be taken home, and Dad, unable to speak any words, crying and patting her on the back. Once Mum has calmed down we spend an hour in the garden, with her happily chatting to us and members of staff, as though she had been there for ever. Endless cups of tea and biscuits appear and staff come and say hello to Dad.

When it is time to leave, the nightmare begins all over again. With Mum clinging to Dad, it is horrific. We prise her fingers off him and gently but firmly push her away from the door so that we can punch in the code without her seeing. Not that she would remember but we're not exactly engaging brain either. With the help of staff who had heard the yelling and hold Mum back we squeeze our way out, making sure the solid door shuts before she can get to it. On some visits we're not fast enough and Mum grabs the door. Again, we have to prise her fingers off and push her away.

As we make our way to the car, we can hear Mum screaming and hammering on the glass, calling my name, shouting abuse. Accusing Dad of abandoning her yet again. We aren't allowed to take Mum out for walks as getting her back into the unit is difficult and, to be honest, dangerous. Every visit finishes with screams of 'GET ME OUT OF HERE! I HATE YOU! I ALWAYS HATED YOU!

Occasionally, other patients have been lurking and, if the door is held open a second longer than necessary to get us out, it becomes a bit of a 'One Flew Over The Cuckoo's Nest' moment when a charge for the door by several in-mates can only be foiled by me shoving Dad through and pulling it shut, with lightning speed behind me.

Sometimes, I then become the 'Bitch From Hell' for Mum AND her friends as they ALL start yelling and banging the glass.

Any sense I had of 'happy ever after' is quickly swept away when I face the mountain of paperwork and meetings between one local authority and another.

For the Bournemouth Local Authority to 'hand' Mum over to the Kingston Local Authority she needed a Kingston address.

To register Mum with a GP in Kingston she needed a Kingston address.

For us to register Mum at a secure care home that specialised in dementia in Kingston she needed a Kingston address.

The race is on to find a new home for Dad in Kingston in both their names. Until we did we must continue to travel back and forth to Bournemouth, visiting Mum at the unit, looking after Dad and packing up sixty years of marriage.

Looking for a secure care home for Mum was more difficult and we quickly discovered that there aren't many secure homes in the country, let alone Surrey.

As we search for a care home, I take advice from the dozens of kind people who have been through similar circumstances. The home mustn't smell of pee. There must be natural light. Colourful rooms and daily activities. A balanced diet and fresh food. The residents shouldn't be sitting around the room wearing a bib, in readiness for the next meal. The residents should be engaging when spoken to, not drugged up to the eyeballs. The residents' bedrooms must be comfortable, with personal belongings and memories, preferably with an en-suite bathroom. If the home has 'preferable' visiting times during the day they should be relaxed with the idea of your popping in as and when.

I'm sure some homes we visited suspected us of being undercover TV reporters as I fired questions at them while Nicky went around sniffing things and chatting to residents.

Having had a conversation with Nicky some weeks before, and her pulling the "Sorry Lizzie but this is too bloody traumatic for me to deal with. I'm going to pull the younger child card", she starts to do what she is really good at. Hour upon hour of internet searches and chats with care homes in the Kingston area, together with finding a retirement flat that might suit Dad, I feel we are moving along as fast as we can. She organises evening and weekend appointments for us and we start to look at places together while trying to fit in visits to both Mum and Dad.

Twenty

The six months anniversary of my moving into Lucy's flat fast approaches. I can't believe it has been this long. I am acutely aware that Lucy couldn't rent out her spare room and, worse still, she wouldn't let me contribute rent-wise. Her 'events' business was really taking off and she needed all the financial help she could get.

Lucy ran her business from home and chaos whirled around the place as she sorted out venues, themes, catering, candles, staff, security, PR, marketing, website, membership vetting and anything else needed to make her Company and the evening a success. There were never ending 'urgent' deadlines as the next party approached and a constant stream of 'hangers-on, desperate to be Lucy's next best friend. It was relentless. Exhausting. Brilliant.

I had entered a pattern of cycle, work, home, weird guests, cook, Mum, Dad, home, sleep; cycle, work, home, weird guests, cook, Mum, Dad, sleep. I started to crave some alone time.

Lucy keeps trying to get me interested in online dating but I'm not ready for that and brush it aside with a barked, "Just drop it!" To be honest it scares me. I've heard so many horror stories from friends and read articles in the newspapers warning of dastardly males scamming vulnerable women out of their life savings, even though I didn't have a pot to piss in, it still worried me.

I know I've made progress. My finances are as settled as I could hope, considering, but I was desperate to have some independence.

To cheer me up, my divorce is finally through and I can add fifty per cent of Williams's Army Pension to my regular income.

I could plan on a place somewhere not too far away and annoy William at the same time, knowing he must be really angry at losing half his pension. Over thirty five years being 'wife of' does sometimes pay off though not necessarily as I might have wished.

Fate must have been on my side when later that week I overhear a conversation at the office one morning between colleagues, one of whom was celebrating saving enough money for a deposit on a house. I shuffled over to her desk.

"How did you manage that?" I asked.

"Housesitting," she replied.

I had no idea what she was talking about.

"Well, I pay six hundred and fifty pounds a month rent to look after this woman's house while she's working in New York. Her son's at boarding school so I'm pretty much there by myself the whole time. They pop back every couple of months, but other than that…"

I could manage six hundred and fifty a month. It would be a stretch but I could do it.

"Is it miles away?"

'Oh, no. Hammersmith."

Twenty minutes bike ride for me.

I'm of the 'if it sounds too good to be true it usually is' as taught at the school of Glass Half Empty. "What's the catch?"

"Erm… There isn't one, really. Just feed four cats and a spider and look after the house."

Spider?

"No wild parties!"

Spider?

"She's back next week. Do you want to meet her? She's hoping I'll find someone, to save her having to find someone."

Spider?

"Yes. That would be great."

I return to my desk. The more I think about this the more I start to love the idea. It would be the perfect solution all round. Privacy and, more importantly, having a *tiny* bit of a life. Albeit a very skint one.

A week later I'm ringing the doorbell on a beautiful London town house. One of those posh four-story things that I've always loved but never dreamed I could own. Maybe I can pretend it's mine when she's away.

Fiona is about my age, blonde, skinny, obviously very successful and very wealthy. I step into the house cautiously, scanning the floor as I make my way to the kitchen, half expecting to tread on a tarantula.

"Are you visually impaired?" she asks me.

"What? Oh, no. I was…" I take a breath. "The spider. Where is it?"

She nods. Dead serious. "Come with me. But don't make any sudden movements, okay?" I nervously follow.

She takes me to her son's room, a shrine to all arachnid related, and leads me to a small glass tank.

"He's in there."

I peer in the tank and eventually make out a hairy blob with legs that seemed to go on for ever.

"Is that it?"

She laughs. "Yes. To be honest the cats are more ferocious. It's a tarantula and they're very hairy, slow moving and boring,"

A *bit like my ex husband.*

"You only need to open up the top of the tank, refresh the water and drop in one or two crickets. Don't worry though as I have a year's supply in the freezer. In some countries they are considered a delicacy."

Well that's me sorted for canapes if I can't afford to shop before the next pay day

Sitting in Fiona's spacious kitchen where all things seem to match beautifully, and drinking out of matching mugs – no "World's Best Mum" ones here that's for sure. She explains that after a lengthy and ugly divorce she kept the house, received a sizeable monthly alimony, and earned a hefty banker's salary.

Ah. Just like me…

We get on well and end up tipsy over supper, cooked by her own fair (perfectly-manicured) hands. We swap divorce stories. Admittedly I make it sound as if I'm only temporarily in 'dire straits' and will eventually get a 'big pay out', even though the divorce has come through. Well, I don't want to sound pathetic or needy. She might think I'll sell the silverware. She understands my predicament and is happy to offer me the room: a converted attic bedroom with en-suite bathroom. It's tiny. It's perfect. I love it. I immediately agree to the six hundred and fifty pounds a month rent and, without thinking, agree *not* to register myself at her address with the local authorities and *not* use her address as my postal address.

I didn't think of the implications until Lucy pointed them out to me when I excitedly tell her that she can have her spare room back.

"You won't be able to get a parking permit at her address. You'll have to leave the battered bitch here."

Shit. I hadn't thought of that.

"The post isn't a big deal. I'll bring it round or you can pick it up."

I do the goldfish thing for a second.

"She doesn't want to pay tax on your rent, Ma. At six hundred and fifty pounds a month she's over the tax-free threshold"

"The what, what?"

"It's not your problem, it's hers."

"But what if she's caught out? Does that make me an accessory to the fact?"

Lucy burst out laughing, "This isn't an episode of The Wire, Ma. Chill out. It's her problem and a pain in the arse for you. But we can work round it."

"But I'll have to schlepp across London to pick up and drop off the car. It's bad enough driving three hours to see Nanny and Granddad. This'll add another hour."

"You are moving forwards. Compared to everything you've already been through the car and post shit is nothing. Right?"

"True. But I'm still not listed anywhere; not paying Council Tax and…"

"And just 'cause you're moving out doesn't mean you can start being a whiny bitch, either." Also, true.

I spend the next few hours throwing my stuff in bin bags, in readiness for the move.

Two weeks later I'm waving Fiona and her son off. I do a few waltzes with my invisible partner throughout the entire downstairs.

I settle in quickly. I have the run of the house but my bedroom is my sanctuary, with my little TV and a kettle on the small side table.

I find out the cats are bloody unfriendly, they've probably got word from Mum's cat that I'm a heartless bitch, with one of them taking up residence on the third step up so that, when coming down, I nearly always trip. The dreaded spider is not so bad as, other than getting Ed to come round once a week to feed and water it, I don't need to go anywhere near it

For the first month, I am drunk on freedom. I make supper at least three times a week for whoever is available:

Jenny, Lucy, Ed, Nicky, work colleagues, friends from the hospital. I am overspending and am brought up short when my cash card is declined at Tesco's by the bejewelled checkout boy.

I am completely settled in my new home and, snuggling under the duvet, happy with the thought that all the animals are fed and cared for (and locked in the house). I settle down for a great night's sleep when my mobile rings. Please, God, don't let it be Mum on the run again. I squint at my phone. William. I let it ring. It eventually stops. My heart rate slows. I drift off. The phone rings again. Fuck's sake! I snatch the phone off the bedside table.

"Yes?"

"Are you awake?"

I hate it when people say that, when you've just answered the sodding phone.

"Of course I'm bloody awake. What do you want?"

William clears his throat, something he always does when he's about to tell me what to do.

"I've heard about the house you've moved into and wondered whether I could come and stay."

I can't believe what I'm hearing.

"I won't be a bother and the owner doesn't need to know I'm there."

The cheeky, pompous twat.

"Are you joking?"

"No."

"What's happened to your Polish 'soul mate'? Has she seen the light?"

"We've fallen out. Things aren't going so well."

I stifle my laughter.

"She put a post-it note on the fridge 'Do not touch my eggs'"

I burst out laughing. I had assumed her eggs were his eggs some time ago and would be, for ever more.

"I'm on the sofa and it's doing my back in," he whines.

"Oh dear. Well, life's a bitch, isn't it? Try the floor."

"Why must you be so difficult, Lizzie?"

"I'm not being 'difficult' William. I'm telling you to fuck off."

"And you wonder why I went elsewhere."

"And if I ever meet your 'soul mate' I'll thank her for taking you off my hands!"

"I think you'll find I got rid of *you*."

That's it. Bored now.

"Shut up! JUST SHUT UP! You're not staying here. EVER! And don't ask me for anything EVER again!"

"You're a selfish bitch…"

I hang up. Angry that William had managed to get a few words in before I did. My heart thuds in my chest. Angry and excited at the same time. I am going up, admittedly at a glacial speed, but William is definitely, going down… and not in the way he hoped for. I laugh at my own dirty joke.

I'm proud of myself. I've moved on. If anything, my life is better and a lot less complicated now I am single. The past ten years of marriage to William had been chaotic, controlling and aggressive. The thought of having to deal with Mum and Dad while still married to him is horrific. I make some tea and toast myself in the mirror "Well done, me."

Twenty-one

Nicky and I visit dozens of flats. Expensive, cramped, in need of renovation, in terrible areas, unfriendly neighbours, so when a two-bedroom retirement flat comes up for sale we practically implode with relief. Minutes away from Nicky and not far from me, walking distance into Kingston town centre and in a block of flats with a beautiful communal garden, overseen by an efficient and friendly manager; it couldn't be better for Dad.

We soon find out why Dad's Bournemouth neighbour has always been so attentive. Unbeknownst to us Dad had agreed to sell him the house way below the asking price and no begging from me and Nicky could get Dad to go back on his 'promise'. We were mortified because we wanted him to have as much money as possible and had no idea yet what fees were expected when a secure place was found for Mum. There was nothing we could do so we just got on with making sure the sale of the Bournemouth house and purchase of the Kingston flat went through as soon as possible. Again, this was not without moments of high drama as the house was in both Mum and Dad's name and we therefore needed Mums signature on all the documents. We talked this through with the staff at her unit who said that it wasn't a problem if she agreed to sign. As yet she had not officially been diagnosed and was still under observation. If she didn't want to sign anything they would not allow us to put pressure on her. After copious amounts of tea and biscuits, and the appearance of pen and paper, Mum signed without any comment. We were on track.

Twenty-Two

Mum, who had mostly lived in Army houses, has trained us in efficient and fast packing. She could pack up and clean an entire house in a week. And when I say clean I mean *clean*. Mum did everything single handed, from hand washing floors, walls, cupboards, carpets and beds. Allocated a specific number of tea boxes (the more senior a rank you were the more boxes you got) she was ruthless about what to pack, and more importantly, how to pack as much stuff in a tiny tea box as possible. As each room was emptied and cleaned it became a no-go area. As each piece of cutlery was polished we were left with one fork, knife, spoon each. Ditto crockery. Ditto clothing.

On 'marching out' day a serious soldier, wearing white gloves to test surfaces for dust, would go through the house; sniffing pillows, lifting mattresses, running his gloved finger along the top of doors, slowly ticking items off the list on his clipboard. Mum would silently watch, daring that soldier to find dirt. He never did find any. I felt sad, watching this soldier walk around the house, peering into every nook and cranny. Did he really sign up to inspect houses? All that learning how to fire a rifle and he was putting his gloved finger inside Mum's hoover.

Having waved off the removal van, Nicky climbs into the back of the car, settling herself next to the cat who is kicking up a storm in the carrier and, with Dad sitting in the passenger seat looking like a terrified driving test instructor, tapping the dashboard and pointing forward, we set out. After five minutes I have to tell Nicky to stop singing to the bloody cat.

"But I'm keeping her calm."

"Well, it's not working!"

What with the singing , Dad constantly pointing at the speedometer or tapping the gear stick, I wouldn't say it was a relaxing journey.

We eventually arrive at the door of Dad's new home. No sooner are we in than Dad's hanging pictures at lightning speed making the place his home. The cat takes advantage of the moment and tears out of the back door, hopefully never to be seen again.

As I start on the unpacking I notice Nicky is nowhere to be seen. Pissed off at the prospect of doing this by myself I go on the hunt and find her in the reception area, reading the flyers on the noticeboard.

"Are you going to help unpack or what?"

Nicky chuckles.

"Have you read these? Dad's not going to get five minutes peace!"

I look at the fliers pinned to the board. Tea dances every Friday, cinema every Wednesday, coffee and cake every Tuesday afternoon, book club every Monday morning and 'Hot Yoga for Arthritics' every Sunday with Tanya in number seven. Her heating bill must be astronomical.

"According to the door bells, nineteen of the twenty one flats are occupied by ladies. The only other man is Mr. Singh in number twelve. I bet he'll be happy to see dad!" Nicky cracks up laughing.

At that moment, a gaggle of highly perfumed ladies of a certain age slowly make their way through the reception area. Nicky and I nod hello. And nod. And nod. It takes them forever to get out of the front door. I'm sure I had whiplash by the time they left.

Dad's finished hammering nails in the wall and has changed his clothes. Grey trousers, white shirt, regimental tie, blazer and highly polished shoes. Immaculate. At over six feet tall, Dad's never left the house without a tie on or his shoes cleaned. He looks every inch the perfectly turned out gent. He doesn't own a t-shirt or trainers and has certainly never worn jeans. The closest he gets to 'casual' is beige trousers and a polo shirt.

Born in Portsmouth and one of nine children, Dad had a very poor upbringing. There were few opportunities for a boy in the mid-1940s and, despite being one year short of the signing up age, he signed up anyway. The choice of regiments was laid out before him in the form of cap badges. He chose the Welsh Guards leek, mistaking it for a palm tree His thinking, on that winter's day, was that it must be a regiment that visited hot countries, (or so he used to tell us). There followed over thirty years of career soldiering.

He was a brilliant social climber and immensely popular with officers and other ranks alike; he was determined to make something of himself. He organised annual Pantomimes and variety shows regardless of where the regiment was posted. He rose through the ranks and reached Captain, remaining friends with almost everyone in the process.

Standing there in his civvies, he hands me a note 'See Mum. My car?'

After what feels like for ever Nicky and I have been bombing down to Bournemouth to see Mum and Dad. Me in the Battered Bitch, which miraculously was still running, and Nicky either taking the train or bus. Dad's Nissan Micra was close in age to the BB and just as unreliable. The thought of taking either car today was out of the question. Nicky and I were exhausted and the thought of letting Dad drive didn't come into it. He'd probably end up back at his old house, completely forgetting the address of the new place

"Let's go shopping!" Nicky yelled, with a big smile on her face that could be interpreted as hysteria.

Dad's hearing had deteriorated recently too, so not only could he not speak, he couldn't hear much either. 'Paper conversations' (as I liked to call Dad's note writing) veered from mortifying to hysterical. On one occasion in a café, when we were served by a particularly pretty waitress, he wrote 'Great legs!' on a piece of paper and passed it to me, not realising the waitress was standing right behind him. She leant over, took the pen and wrote 'Thanks!'

Nicky and I took Dad around the local area, introducing him to shop owners, informing them of Dad's speech problems and that he was a bit deaf. Most people were kind, some embarrassed, unused to such open and honest communication. One or two were seriously lacking in community spirit and responded with disinterest. It was as if we were asking them to visit Dad on a daily basis and give him a bath.

We spent the next few weeks driving to and from Bournemouth. Now, without the benefit of staying over at Mum and Dad's house, it was a seven hour drive in total; with the trauma of visiting Mum in the middle and comforting Dad for the entire drive back to Kingston. We couldn't just drop him off at his flat; we had to settle him in, give him supper, then sit with him while he ate. Lately he was prone to choking if the food wasn't cut up properly. Recent mini strokes had affected his ability to swallow. We felt guilty leaving him after making sure he'd taken a sleeping tablet and his anti-depressants. It took us a couple days to recover by which time it was time to drive down to Bournemouth again.

Nicky and I had found the perfect care home for Mum. It was secure, homely and had a huge garden. Each room had a picture of the resident on the door so that they didn't get too confused. The staff were respectful and more than we could hope for. Overall we felt a feeling of safety, laughter and friendliness. Firstly, the care home had to accept Mum as a new resident and, after much pleading, agreed to visit Mum in Bournemouth to assess her. Incredibly they agreed and, even more incredibly Mum was on form that day.

The only setback was that the home was full. We would have to wait for a bed to become available. Or, as Nicky subtly put it, "Wait for a resident to drop off their perch." This could be next week, month or even year. The thought of a year of driving to Bournemouth brought about bizarre conversations with Nicky suggesting we have one of the residents 'knocked off'. We were that desperate but we were joking of course. Well, I was. I wasn't sure about Nicky.

Mum was now registered at Dad's address. We had a sticky moment with the manager of Dad's flat who, knowing that we were trying to get Mum into a home nearby, was unsure that Dad's flat could be considered as Mum's home as she hadn't lived there. It was such a frustrating time. Just when we finally had everything falling into place something as ridiculous as this was getting in the way. We argued the flat was in both their names so it shouldn't be a problem. And it was also not really his business.

Once contracts were signed for the retirement flat, we could sign on with a local GP and move Dad in. The GP would not take Mum on until she had been moved to Kingston

After four long, painful months, a place became available at the care home. Mum was 'released' by Bournemouth council over to Kingston council's healthcare.

It was a beautiful summer's day when I drove Dad to Bournemouth to pick Mum up. As usual, she's waiting at the door with her bags packed, just as she has been every time we have visited. We'd find all sorts in her bag. Someone else's teeth, reading glasses, watch, ring. Sometimes she'd even be dressed in someone else's clothes with the staff smiling, telling us "We tried to get her changed but she wouldn't have it."

I have no idea if the excitement Mum expresses at leaving the secure unit is 'real'. She is excited but, to be honest, the reason for that could be anything from the fact that she's wearing someone else's shoes or that she's going on a 'journey'. Her mood could change from happy to despairing to angry from one second to the next. There was every chance she could throw herself out of my car on the M3 *or* sleep the entire way.

I didn't care what her excitement was based on; I was just relieved she was excited and not trying to kill me. For a joyous moment, Dad was Mum's hero as he led her by the hand to my car. They couldn't stop kissing each other like two naughty children.

On the way to Kingston we stopped for tea at a service station on the M3. Normally this would be a fraught undertaking but today, with Mum comfortable in Dad's company, it was such a joyful experience; with Mum holding Dad's hand and Dad patting Mum reassuringly.

It made me wonder if everything could go back to 'normal'. Maybe Mum could live with Dad. Maybe she didn't need to go into a care home. And maybe pigs could fly, as I spotted Mum waltzing out of the shop with her pockets bulging with stolen goods. But she was happy; that was the main thing. I did pay for them by the way.

The rest of the journey was uneventful. Mum fell asleep in the back of the car, with her head resting on Dad's shoulder, with Dad giving me the thumbs up in the rear view mirror.

As we pull up at the care home, Mum seems to sense what is coming. My stomach had been in knots the entire way. I knew the transition wouldn't be smooth. I knew that in Mum's eyes she was exchanging one 'prison' for another.

Nicky had picked up ornaments, pictures and clothes from Dad's flat for Mum's room and was now waiting in the care home's garden. They'd laid out tea and cake in preparation for Mum's arrival.

I persuaded Mum to get out of the car and just have a look.

"Promise you won't leave me here?" she asked.

"Promise," I lied (again). But what could I do? I had to get her in and Dad was already getting upset.

We enter the home, Mum is welcomed by staff and led to the garden, where Nicky is waiting.

We have tea, cake, tears and laughter but, inevitably, the awful moment arrives when we have to take Mum to her room. No amount of soft furnishings, pictures on walls, flowers in the garden or kindly staff was going to make it any better for Mum. In her confused mind, she was being abandoned again and I knew nothing I said or did was going to change that. She fought to leave the room, then the corridor, then the home.

Once again we had to sneak out of the care home, the staff distracting Mum, who was weeping and begging to be let out. She just wanted to go home. She wanted her mum.

None of us had the strength to speak as we drove back to Dad's flat. We are exhausted, broken and deeply sad. It had taken two years to get to this point. From Mum going walkabout and Dad having his strokes, we had now managed to get them both into secure homes, closer to us. If only we could say, "It'll all be fine now." but we couldn't. We knew it wouldn't ever be "fine". It was only going to get worse.

Twenty-Three

Meanwhile, back at Spider Ranch, things were deteriorating rapidly. Fiona has thrown in her job in New York, taken her son out of boarding school and both were now living in the house full time, which is fine; it's their home after all. But any hope of this being an Ab Fab type friendship, two middle aged single women getting on like a house on fire while the studious son rolls his eyes at them, is far from the truth. We were so completely different.

Fiona and her son bicker from the moment they get up to the moment they go to bed and even then, they sometimes continue to bellow at one another through the wall. I absolutely refuse (in my head) to step in, even when I get caught in the cross fire. I have enough to be getting on with looking after Mum and Dad. And me.

Fiona's son missed his friends (and father) and Fiona was rudderless, having left an amazing job abroad. In my opinion she hadn't left her job in New York of her own accord, based on the fact that she rattled out a hundred different reasons why she left. Madam protesteth too mucheth me thinketh. Me thinketh she was booted outeth.

After almost two years as a single woman of insufficient means and now happily living in someone else's big town house, I was finally enjoying life and Fiona didn't like that. The house had been my brilliant sanctuary for a year; all through Mum being in the secure unit, Dad moving into his new flat, right up until Mum moved into the lovely care home. The peace and quiet I enjoyed after work, reading, watching TV or working on my laptop was no more.

Things got worse following a visit from Ed who, surprised that Fiona answered the door, swept in with a "Oh, hi! I'm Ed. Is Ma upstairs?" He then took the stairs, two at a time, without waiting for permission. There followed, from Fiona's point of view, lots of unexplained laughter which she probably thought was about her.

Despite Ed only staying for half an hour Fiona insisted afterwards that I meet friends and family outside the house in future. She said her son found 'visitors' disruptive.

Her controlling behaviour continued for days and she then started adding 'duties' for me. For example, show her son how to cook by 'perhaps' preparing an evening meal for him if she was working late; 'perhaps' help her son with his homework. I kind of felt obliged to help; Fiona was in a bad place and maybe, eventually, she'd settle into her new (lower salaried) job and cheer the fuck up. But things didn't change and I felt she was deliberately trying to grind me down.

If I wasn't visiting Mum or Dad I'd visit Lucy, Jenny or Ed straight after work or, if they weren't available, I'd sit in a pub with a book and glass of wine or go out for after work drinks with colleagues, just so that I didn't get home before Fiona. When I did finally roll in I'd say a quick 'Hi!' then head straight upstairs to my room to watch TV with my head phones on. I must have lost at least half a stone purely on running up the stairs and not bothering to go to the kitchen for a snack.

"Would you like me to move out?" I asked one evening, bolstered by the courage of after work gin and tonics.

"No! Of course not. I like having a lodger." I interpreted that as meaning she liked having a six hundred and fifty pounds in her bank account, because she clearly didn't like *me*.

Lucy, Jenny and Ed knew what was going on, of course, and were told not to come to the house unless it was an absolute emergency. However, they could see how miserable this whole situation was making me.

I'd just returned home from work, managing to avoid some awful conflict going on in the bathroom, and settled down to TV with headphones when Lucy suddenly burst into my room. Fiona was right behind her, a thunderous look on her face.

"Sorry, emergency. Family only," Lucy said, as she shut the door in Fiona's face.

I bolted out of bed, almost garrotting myself on the headphones. "What's happened? Who's hurt? Is anyone dead?"

Lucy giggles. "No. Nothing's wrong." She gives me a kiss, plonks herself on my bed, fishes a bottle of wine and two glasses out of her cavernous bag and logs onto my computer. Is nothing sacred?

"How would you describe your personality?"

"Oh, um... Positive? Happy?"

"Cool. How about '*Fun loving divorcee seeking likeminded for a good time?*"

"What? Is this for one of your naughty parties or something?"

"Nope! It's for you. I've signed you up for online dating. I need to do the personality bit."

"No! I don't want to! Take me off it!"

"Nope. You're on and staying on. You don't have to do anything or go out with anyone or meet anyone." Lucy gives me a flat stare. "The state you're in right now I'd be surprised if you got *any* interest whatsoever."

"I was in bed!" I rush to the mirror. I do look like shit.

"So, 'Fun loving divorcee...'"

"You make me sound like an old tart!"

"What then?"

After an exhausting half an hour, where I had flash backs of form filling for Mum's care home and Dad's house sale, Lucy finished with a flourish. She stabbed at a few keys then...I was LIVE. Complete with photos and details.

"Recently divorced, fun loving, seeks like-minded person for cinema, theatre, meals out and lots of laughter".

Lucy said, "Let's see what happens." She gave me a hug, thundered down the stairs, shouting "Goodnight chaps" to the rest of the house and left.

I slammed the laptop screen down, then pulled the plug from the wall just to be sure. Because I *still* believed there was some sort of 'juice' flowing from the computer through the socket, and by juice I didn't mean the electrical kind. I meant the magic, possibly green kind. Just to be extra safe I put the laptop in a drawer. Switched the light out and went to bed.

The next morning I lay in bed, staring at the drawer with the laptop in it.

"For God's sake."

I retrieve the laptop and open the dating site. Standing there, in my penguin T-shirt, looking at a whole heap of strangers who were, in turn, looking back at me. The smiley one, the sultry one, the angry one, the boring one.

I slammed the lid down again and jumped in the shower. Ignoring them was the best thing to do. They'd go away then. I wouldn't open the site again. Ever.

Twenty-Four

With Fiona and son back in the house every bit of freedom I had managed to find for myself after moving out of Lucy's seemed to be taken away. I'd found a happy-ish medium of work, visiting Mum and Dad, seeing the children and finding time for myself. I had no money to spare, so my luxury was time. Time to visit galleries, time to go for long walks, time to read. But now that time has been taken from me.

I'd stupidly mentioned that Lucy had signed me up to an online dating site. Not one to be outdone, Fiona also signs up to the same site and is much quicker off the mark. She's on a mission to find a man and agrees to a date with every man that has the misfortune to hone into view. She uses me as her ad-hoc babysitter. This doesn't mean me just staying in, which I don't have too much of a problem with, but as well as the cooking lessons and homework checking, it now includes running a bath for her son aged 14.

One evening, after I'd just dropped a dead cricket in the spider's tank, whilst the son was wallowing in the bath, I hear Fiona come home. She'd only been gone an hour, on some date with a 'marvellous' man she'd met online. Maybe she's forgotten something. Her personality, perhaps.

I peer over the banister, listening to her slamming kitchen cupboard doors. Something was clearly 'up'.

I find Fiona in the kitchen. She's on the wine and very pissed off.

"How did the date go?" I ask.

"Fucking awful."

"Oh no! What happened?" I said, full of genuine concern. Maybe if Fiona got shagged until her eyes rolled into the back of her head she'd be happier. I know. I'm being stupid, right?

"He said I was too aggressive and demanding!"

"No-o-o-o!" Yessss. You arrrrrre.

"I mean, Christ, let's be honest, that's why they go on this bloody website. To sleep around."

I nod while surreptitiously pouring wine into my tea mug.

"That's probably why you haven't had any response yet. They know you're not going to give out."

I nod along as she continues to blame every living soul but herself and decide then and there to start responding to a date or two; coffee only…

Twenty-Five

Dad is now taking the bus to see Mum, which takes a heap of pressure off Nicky and me. We take turns to accompany him on the bus, just to let the drivers know why Dad couldn't speak and generally reassure ourselves that Dad knew what he was doing. The care home told us that they didn't have a problem with his visiting on a daily basis; they could see it calmed Mum down (most of the time) and made their lives easier; and they didn't mind the free lunch he had. I should think not. It was costing enough.

Mum's behaviour at the home, when we visited, had become a pattern too. She was usually tearfully happy to see whoever turned up. There'd be cuddles, as she sat by the front door, bags packed, waiting for her mum to take her home. Then she'd get angry as we tried to coax her away from the door, fearful that her mum wouldn't find her if she wasn't waiting by the door. We resort to all kinds of deception.

If I'm on my own, I rely on "Fancy a fag, Mum?" to get her away from the door and out into the garden.

If it's too cold or raining we take shelter in the shed, sit on wobbly garden chairs and puff away, as if we're bunking off school. It must have looked funny from the care home – puffs of smoke coming out of that tiny shed.

Mum loves gardening and although she wasn't allowed to plough her way through the manicured lawns she did 'dead head' the flowers with gusto (whether they were dead or not) and 'break up the earth' with her fingers; which just meant she wanted to get her hands muddy.

The care home manager, Patricia, says it's too early to take Mum out anywhere. She needed to be more settled, institutionalised if you like, before they could take her out for a couple of hours.

On longer visits at the weekend, I would plug Mum into my ipod so that she could listen to songs I had downloaded. This had the most amazing impact on her and we would laugh, listening to her singing along just a bit too loudly. Benny Hill's 'Ernie, the Fastest Milkman in the West' always had her laughing away as though she was hearing it for the first time.

Despite our keeping our side of the bargain, in Mum's head, no such rules applied. She managed to escape more than once.

Even in this ultra-secure home Mum managed to get out. We're talking at *least* three coded doors between her room and the main door, also coded. Nicky and I are secretly proud of Mum's Colditz approach to her incarceration. She'd convince innocent workmen, there to fix plumbing or some electrical fault, that she had been visiting a relative and, with her arms full of other residents' belongings, she'd ask them to open the door for her. Or she'd catch them just as they were leaving and walk right behind them, grabbing the door before it shut.

Patricia would notice her absence quickly, probably because there was no smoke coming from the shed, and alert the police.

She'd quickly be found, usually not far away, chatting with a mechanic in the nearby Kwik Fit or 'helping' a traffic warden put a ticket on a car. On one occasion, she boarded a bus to Putney High Street. Completely alone and terrified; she was looking for her babies again.

The police are brilliant. Having been alerted on other occasions, they knew Mum's name and calmly offered to give her a lift home, even telling her (if that's what it took) that her mum was worried about her and waiting at home. Honestly, all sense of morality went out the window when it came to getting Mum back into a secure place. Being used to doing as she was told by someone in a uniform, Mum went along quietly, chatting away about whatever popped into her head.

Bizarrely, my relationship with Mum is the best it's ever been. It is, in a way, the only positive thing about her dementia. She's more loving, honest and hysterically funny.

I'd never had a close relationship with my Mother. Everything I did annoyed her. Sometimes I put it down to shyness on her part, at other times I assumed the closeness I had to my Dad made her jealous. I could talk to Dad about anything. I couldn't with Mum. But now, sitting in the tiny shed smoking our fags Mum would happily gossip away. Not much of it made sense but we were connected.

"There was another orgy last night." Mum's eyes slide in my direction, as she takes a drag on her fag.

"No-o-o-o. I hope you didn't join in!"

"Nah! Filthy beggers. All over each other, they were. Like dogs."

Mum leans in close and tells me, in a stage whisper

"They were even doing it up the bum."

"No-o-o-o!" I whispered back.

"Disgusting."

I'd nod, philosophically, in a 'these things happen' kind of way.

"And you know, all those boys in the kitchen want to *do it* with me."

"Do they?"

"Oh yes. I have to fight them off with a stick."

Again, I nod along.

"Honestly, Lizzie, I'm so tired. I try to get to sleep but they keep coming in. It's like being in one of those zombie films! I had to ask them to form an orderly queue."

I manage to stifle a snort of laughter.

"Have you told the Boss?" The 'Boss' was the care home manager.

"Oh no, I can't tell her! She's in on it. She organises everything. How do you think she can afford this place?"

On my way out I always update Patricia on what she had been up to the night before.

"You've been at it again haven't you?!"

"Oh No. What now?"

Going home time is always traumatic though. Sometimes I'm tempted to take her to Dad's flat so that she can spend an afternoon with him in the comfort of their own home, surrounded by things she knows. But getting her back to the care home would be horrendous.

"I have to go now, Mum."

I brace myself for the tears and the begging.

"Well, sod off then. I've got stuff to do as well, you know." I laughed all the way to the car. I just couldn't get over the words coming out of her mouth.

Most of the time though, if I take too long saying goodbye, or stay chatting to staff, Mum will end up at the window shouting for me to come back.

After one such visit I could quite easily have punched someone. Luckily, I didn't have to do this because along came a car driver with attitude. Half way home in the BB a very helpful lorry driver tapped on the roof and said

"Did you know your tyres are dangerously flat?"

I could only think to say "Thanks" and then start to hyperventilate.

Tyres? Shit! I'd never had to pump up tyres. How difficult can it be?

I found the nearest garage and pulled up at what I thought was the 'air thing'. It had a hose and words on it. It could have been written in Russian for all the sense it made. I read and re-read what I was meant to do, checked the book in the glove compartment, but still couldn't work it out. I was terrified that I'd do the wrong thing – completely flatten the tyres or put too much air in and they'd explode. A car pulled up behind me and beeped its horn. I waved at them to 'go round'. They beeped again.

The guy in the car was raising his hands in the air and yelled out of his window

"It's not rocket science."

Yes it bloody is. I got out of my car and approached him. Fear swept across his face like an incoming tide. Red faced mad woman of a certain age approaching.

"You have two choices here," I yelled.

"Either shut up and wait or get out and help. You choose but stop the bloody beeping."

He switched his engine off, got out, slammed his door and came over to see what the problem was.

"Why the hell can't your husband do it if you don't know what you're doing?"

"Because he ran off with a Polish woman, took all my money, left me with nothing, I only have this car left and if you don't want to help then GO AWAY."

Silence, apart from the hum of traffic and the sound of my own heart thumping in my ears, terrified he'd punch me, or worse still, not sort my tyres out. He apologised, put air in the tyres, checked the oil and water and asked me if I was okay to fill the tank up. I thanked him profusely. I've never seen anyone drive off so quickly. He didn't even put air in his own tyres.

I still don't understand how to pump up a tyre and feel slightly queasy when I look at the machine in a petrol station. That's not being a dumb blonde. That's being too "busy" to understand the tyre pressure. That's my excuse and I'm sticking to it.

Twenty-Six

I have opened the laptop. I have logged onto the dating website. I have acknowledged that the sultry/boring/angry/idiotic photos of various males between the ages of fifty five and sixty five are still there with accompanying emojis. I have decided to go on a few dates. As previously stated, the subject will attend coffee meetings only.

With the excitement of an imminent gynaecological procedure, I respond to one or two of the less cretinous looking of the bunch. Harsh, I know, but to be honest, I'm still not a fan of the opposite sex and I'm doing this mainly to piss Fiona off. And I acknowledge I need to get over what Lucy calls my 'cock block'.

"I don't want to," I insist.

"I know that, but you have to start at least liking men again or you'll never get near a cock again."

"Sounds fine to me." I respond, petulantly.

So, along with the 'annoy Fiona by dating' and 'get over cock block' I could add 'shut Lucy up."

COFFEE 1

I inform everyone in the office that I'm going on a coffee date with someone I've met online. Having had several late night events, I am allowed to take time off in lieu so I don't feel guilty at all. Once the whoops and wolf whistles cease I give everyone said dates profile.

"Mr Reliable is six feet tall. Brown eyes, hair thinning. Likes cinema, theatre, dogs etc."

I leave the office at nine fifty five in the morning to a warming round of applause and shouts of 'Merde!' and 'Break a leg!'. I feel like Judy Dench about to take to the stage as Elizabeth I. I manage to hold back on the queenly wave.

I arrive at the café at ten o'clock exactly. The six foot man is in fact five foot seven. I almost slap him when he leans in for a sniff and declares "mmm. You smell like my ex-wife."

Ten fifteen I return to the office to cheers and laughter.
"NEXT!" I shout.

COFFEE 2

"Stargazer is five foot ten tall, blue eyes, bald, likes… "Again, I leave the office at nine forty five to cheers and applause. How long will this support last, I ask myself? What do I do when they get bored? Cheer myself out the door?

I arrive at ten precisely. Yes, Stargazer is indeed five foot ten and yes, he's very bald. He's also bonkers. He's pre-ordered my cappuccino, knowing that I'm on my break, and we sit on stools facing out onto the main road and people watch. After the preliminary 'Nice to meet you' he reveals himself. No, not that way, but it was just as jaw dropping.

"You have to keep a look out for weaklings," he informs me. "There are forces out there, you know."

R-i—i-i-g-h-t. I look at the people walking past, fast paced, to and from whatever busy life they are leading.

"No!" He grabs my arm.

"Don't make eye contact! That's how they know!"

"Know what?" I asked, staring at the ground.

He looked at me with disdain "What do you think?"

I shake my head. Someone please rescue me. Alien, human, I don't care right now.

"They'll *know*. What you're thinking, where you're going. It's *vital* that you change your daily routine as much as possible. Throw them off the scent."

Thankfully my mobile started to ping. Messages from work colleagues

"Where are you?"

"How's it going?"

"He must be a good one!"

"Are you dead in a ditch? If so can I have your office?"

Well, time flies when you're with a tin foil hat wearer. I'd been there an hour!

I made my excuses and left, making sure not to make eye contact until I got back to the office.

COFFEE 3

"Online name is 'FatController'. He's five foot ten", bald, interested in reading and shopping."

"Maybe he's gay!" says Paul, "Maybe I should come with you, to be sure. Y'know, protection."

"Maybe not," I reply.

I leave the office at nine forty five to a muted round of applause. The excitement is wearing off amongst my colleagues. How do they think I feel?

I arrive at the café at ten precisely. William is sitting in the corner, back to the wall. In case any Russian spies happen to be passing, he's ready.

Yes, okay, I'd lied to my colleagues but if I'd told them the truth they would have nailed me to my desk.

William had called me the night before declaring he needed to see me about something money related.

"Good financial or bad financial?" I asked. I don't know why I did ask,. I can only ever be bad where William is concerned. I've learnt that much.

He smiles, stands as I approach, holds a chair out of me. I deduce that given this courteous overkill he is going to ask for something. I put my money on money.

"You're looking very well, Mrs.Watkins." He revelled in the fact that I still had my married name and hadn't reverted to my maiden name. Trust me, it was down to pure idleness and convenience.

"What's the drama?" I get straight to the point. I'm past being polite.

His mobile pings. He checks the message. Replies.

"The soul mate?" I ask, keeping my voice light.

Without looking up William replies "No. She moved out."

"Sorry. Did you say she's moved out? Oh, dear. That's terrible. And it all seemed so… permanent."

This goes over William's head. Maybe the text message is a death threat. Maybe I should let them know where he is. Maybe I should offer to do him in myself. I wonder how much I'd get paid.

William finally puts his phone down, clears his throat. I brace myself. He is about to tell me what to do. Again.

"Well, Mrs Watkins, it's been two years now, and clearly we have both… had time to come to terms with our separation and the fact that we are both struggling to cope without each other, as, no doubt, are our children."

William continued to deal with his phone each time it pinged as I zoned out. I couldn't bear to listen to him. Nothing he could say would be of interest until that is I heard the words 'back' and 'together' and 'forgiveness'.

"Did you just say forgiveness?" I ask.

He clears his throat and does this sickly 'you're a very naughty girl' laugh.

"Yes, I have seen your 'profile' on a sex dating site." Laugh laugh laugh. Twat.

PING. Read. Reply.

"It's not a *sex* dating site. It's a *dating* site." I wonder who has told him. Oh God, what if he's joined?

"Have you signed up?" Damn, I wish I hadn't asked. I wish I'd been cool and laid back and not given a shit.

He smiles at me. Patronising git. That sickly laugh again.

PING. Read. Reply.

"And by the way, I don't want you back. I'd rather give myself paper cuts and swim in the sea."

PING. Read. Reply.

I snatch his mobile off him and drop it in the jug of water on the table next to ours. The people sitting at the table seemed as pleased as I was. The pinging phone was driving them mad too.

Any doubt I may have had about my decision not to take William back is swept away the moment he jumps to his feet and screams in my face.

"YOU MAD COW! What will it take for you to trust me again?"

I'm the mad cow? I beg to differ.

As I make my way back to the office I decide it is time to try an after work 'meal date'. Just to piss William off. And Fiona. And give my colleagues a break.

I was back at my desk by ten thirty. I had an email from my new boss. She's only been here a month and already she's pissed everyone off, She not only 'single-handedly' raised millions at her last job but also had a degree that she'd 'won' at a fancy University which, in my day, had been called a 'Polytechnic. She had surrounded herself with incredibly clever young people who remained in 'the back room' so I had my suspicions about her personal capabilities.

We all know she's been brought in to oversee the biggest funding appeal ever undertaken by the hospital and we all know, come hell or high water, she was going to claim ALL the glory. No "I'd like to thank the team" speech is ever going to cross this woman's lips.

During her first staff meeting she homes in on me.

"Hello Lizzie"

"Hi boss. Welcome to the hospital"

She tilts her head to the side and gives me a patronising smile. I know that move. I use it on Mum when she's at peak mental. I make a note not to do it to Mum ever again.

"I know you've carried the 'rock' of responsibility for such a long time, but I'm here now."

She stands before me, arms outstretched. For a second I think she's coming in for a hug until a colleagues hisses

"Pass her the 'rock."

I look at my colleague, she mimes handing over a rock.

"Oh!" I hand over the invisible 'rock' with as much Marcel Marceau finesse as I can muster.

"Thank you Lizzie,"

Head tilt, smile. Cow.

The moment New Boss takes 'the rock' from me my work life turns to shit.

I am inexplicably excluded from meetings. Projects I'm working on disappear from my desk. I don't receive any emails informing me about meetings. I am not included in 'off site' meetings with people that I had a good working relationship with. I am not updated on events I am not organising myself.

I am ordered not to contact hospital staff directly but to ask her permission first.

This entails explaining why I need to contact them in the first place. She would, of course, deny me permission.

I find out later that as soon as I leave her office she would contact them herself, presenting whatever idea I've had as her own.

I've always worked closely with hospital staff but now I was practically invisible.

The boss tells me I need to go on a course because I don't know how to answer the phone properly. Apparently answering the phone with just my name isn't good enough. She demands I say the name of the hospital, followed by department, followed by my whole name and end with 'How can I help you?' by which time the Consultant or donor calling me would very often swear and hang up.

My office colleagues can see what is going on but they decide to take the easy path and not to speak to me when the boss is around. Shame on them.

I can't eat or sleep properly, worrying about this woman and how I can try to make things work. I have imaginary conversations with her in the middle of the night. I even call one of Lucy's Life Coach friend's for tips on body language and non-threatening ways to stand and speak. Still I cannot get it right.

I talk to people I trust. Is it me? Am I going mad or is she just a bitch? I manage to squeeze out some very honest answers. My boss thinks I am a waste of time and space; that I am too posh; that I am not University educated and my methods no longer fit with hospital policy. Well now I know

The time for my annual Appraisal comes and goes. I wait until the end of the day before approaching my boss. She was in her office, stroking the cat on her lap. Not really. That's just how I envisage her in my middle of the night rantings. She was actually just sitting at her desk, typing something vitally important on her computer.

"Hi boss. Sorry to bother you but I am just wondering when I will be having my Appraisal".

She stopped typing and looked over the top of her fake glasses.

"I was hoping you'd just go away".

I reel inside; I feel winded. Thankfully I don't physically respond.

"I've been here a very long time and, do you know, I think I'll still be here long after you have left."

I can tell she wasn't expecting that by the rapid blinking behind the fake glasses.

Of course I feel good after that quip. At least I got one dig back at her. I've thrown down the gauntlet and gained territory. I've rammed my flag in her mound. That sounds terrible but you know what I mean.

I've made things a whole lot worse.

The next day I arrive at the team meeting. To be fair, I don't have much to update people on, what with over half my projects having been taken from me, but I do have some new and exciting possible donor clients to talk about.

Eventually my turn comes and, on the pretext of needing the loo, my boss leaves the room. I know what she is doing. Everyone knows what she is doing. The room falls silent as she closes the door behind her.

"Sorry. Can everyone just give me a minute while I sort through my notes" I say.

I shuffle my papers and pretend to organise myself. I sense the nervousness of my colleagues. They are nothing compared to my own. But I am not going to let that woman win. The silence is painful.

My boss returns to the room looking happy and triumphant.

"Oh good. You're back".

Tilting my head and smiling.

"Let's start with my first and very exciting new donor…"

Damn. I wish I had a camera to capture the look on her face. For a moment, I think she is going to slap me, but she has no alternative but to sit down and listen. It is that or leave the room again.

It is another small victory. I know she is going to make my work life even more uncomfortable. And so begins a period I call "The Great Ignoring". She makes me invisible, not only to herself but her intimidation of others forces them to do the same. My grandfather told me never to 'hate' anyone but just 'dislike' them. I truly hate this woman. I doubt my ability to do anything, including think for myself. I've been working here for over five years now and for the first time I'm starting to dread coming into work.

Twenty-Seven

I slam the small silver ball into the other four silver balls with such force that the entire Newton's Cradle toy flies off the desk at the precise moment the nice looking but frazzled doctor enters the room. He must be good because he doesn't bat an eye.

"Morning Mrs Watkins".

Nice looking Australian doctor. I put the cradle thing back on his desk.

"Sorry. Morning".

Doctor Frazzle sits at his desk, sighs heavily and addresses his computer.

"How can I help?"

"Are you asking the computer or me?"

Poor guy.

He's probably got a pile of problems himself. Maybe he's married to a demanding wife and they've got kids or a new baby and he's knackered. But I'm on this side of the desk. He turns to look at me.

"Sorry. How can I help *you*?"

"I've reached the end of my tether. I didn't have much tether to start with but now I'm at the end of it"

"Ok. Do you want to tell me a little bit about…"

"My husband of thirty five years left me for a Polish masseuse. She was his soul mate apparently. I say "was" because she's left him now. I've just divorced the shit. I've lost everything; money, house, belongings, credit rating, credit cards. I can barely afford to eat. I'm living in a room in a house owned by a mental woman who keeps a spider and argues with her son, who, by the way, is fourteen and can't run his own bath.

On top of all that, my new boss hates me and bullies me every day. She ignores me. She's made everyone ignore me. I've been there 5 years and now I can't bear to go in! She handed me an invisible rock!

I take a breath.

"Blimey. If I were you I'd just leap out of this window here," says Dr Frazzle.

"What?"

He smiles. Joker. We're on the ground floor. What good would that be?

"Sorry, I know I shouldn't have said that but you do seem to have a lot on your plate."

"I haven't told you about my parents yet."

"Oh, you've got some of those too?"

"Sort of. One's got dementia. She's in a care home. Dad can't speak. He's in a retirement flat. I visit both. A lot. All week. And weekends.

"Right. Well. That's a lot of stuff to be dealing with right there."

"And my daughter's signed me up to an on-line dating site…"

He holds his hands up.

"Whoa! Let's get you on something that will help you see the wood from the trees."

"What does that even mean? Wood from the trees?"

"Well I'm no lumberjack but it means that instead of getting stuck on the details, we should focus on the whole."

I love you.

Dr Frazzle suggests anti-depressants.

"No. I'm not depressed."

"Of course you're not. And I'm Mary Poppins."

I agree to pop the pills for three months.

"One other thing," Dr Frazzle says, before I leave

"You should talk to someone about the bullying. HR. Managing Director. Someone trustworthy. You don't want to lose your job on top of everything else."

I leave the doctor's surgery a little more positive than when I arrived.

I start taking the tablets and, after a couple of weeks, certainly start to feel calmer. I decide to try and turn things around by visiting my ex boss, Shirley.

Desperate, I turn up unannounced at her office. I'm surprised she's there and even more surprised she lets me in looking the way I do. I have no control over the snot inducing tears that flow unheeded as she sits me down and pours me a shot of brandy (medicinal)

"Tell me everything." she says.

In between sobs, nose blowing and sipping my medicine, I go through what has happened, leaving nothing out. She's brilliant. Although I knew there was no going back now. I could be out of a job. I could be called a liar. That was my worst fear but I was determined that something had to be done. I had reached rock bottom, felt I had no friends left in the hospital and needed help.

Shirley told me to sit tight and left the office to see her boss, the CEO. They were incredible and, after a meeting with my hideous boss things settled down a little.

When someone touches you in an inappropriate way in the workplace, you report them. If it continues, they can be sacked. Worse case, you could even report them to the police and it can be taken from there.

When you're bullied at work it's very difficult to know what to do. You wonder if you're being a "wimp", a bit pathetic. Will you be labelled a trouble maker. Should you just get a grip and suck it up?

Over time your confidence is whittled away. You feel worthless. You doubt everything you do and every decision you make. You take time off work. You have health issues. You have breakdowns. Suicidal thoughts. Maybe you end up being "paid off" – "Here's some money, now go away." Bullies should be labelled as such. It's in their nature, for whatever reason. Obviously they need help, but until they get that help, others should be warned.

Later that day I am moved to a new office in the main hospital building. I can finally work on events, meet patients who are interested in running their own events, and more or less carry on as before. I even get to see colleagues when I need to. I spend a lot of time on my own. It isn't ideal but the bullying has stopped and I still have my job.

I think the biggest shock for me isn't so much the bullying but how one toxic individual can affect an entire team. I can sort of understand it. Most of the team are young and, being young, don't know how to deal with a deeply insidious individual like my boss. They worry about their jobs; in some cases it is their first serious job. But if anything, I need my job even more. The likelihood of my walking into another job would be unlikely, despite my experience. Apart from that it is the only constant thing in my life, apart from my children, and I have fought to save it.

As in all office environments news filters down through the grapevine. I find out my boss has been given a formal warning. She's certainly behaving in a more professional manner towards me but I can't tell you how huge the relief is when, following the appeal (which raised the fifty million pounds) my boss leaves the building for good. No doubt taking sole credit for the success to her next job.

Twenty-Eight

Nicky and I are finally allowed to take mum out on a regular basis. We start with a couple of hours now and then, then build to whole afternoons; as long as we get her back an hour before teatime. We learn that taking her out one on one isn't a good idea. She'll walk off and, like a head strong three year old, refuse to come back. You know that moment as a parent when you are sprinting along the road and yelling for your (running child) to STOP and not cross the main road. Well that was Mum. With two of us there will be two pairs of eyes watching her skitter around the car park/shop/café.

Every 'journey' brought its own little surprises, like the time Mum tried to pay for a skirt at M and S with cold sausages she'd taken from the care home kitchen. I'll never forget the lady at the till; she didn't bat an eyelid, took one sausage, handed the rest back in 'change' and bagged the skirt. She then waited for Nicky to take Mum to the shoe section while I quickly paid. The till lady kept the sausage though. She said she couldn't wait to hand it in when they balanced the till at the end of the day.

We went on a few outings with both Mum and Dad but these were few and far between. It was too stressful looking after two 'mad' inviduals. Dad was still physically very strong and wasn't one to be gently led anywhere. He'd shove and push us if we didn't go the way he wanted. It was also doubly traumatic getting Mum back in the home, with Dad meowing like a kitten when the time to say goodbye came and Mum, having got accustomed to her five minutes of freedom, refused to leave the car. Sometimes Nicky and I just wanted to lock them in the car and go to the pub for half an hour.

Mum could never settle with a jigsaw or sit with the other 'old people' while listening to some hapless individual play a cheap keyboard and sing wartime songs. She wasn't old, she was young and young meant working. Mum loved working. She'd worked in Administration at Peter Jones, The Army & Navy Store, British Legion and, much more exotically, as a Housing Officer in an ex-pat compound in Saudi Arabia.

She needed to be kept busy and made to feel useful so the care home gave Mum a job in the office. Duties included shredding paper, moving paper and folding paper. All was going well until Mum started to shred documents that she shouldn't have. She also started to complain about her 'salary'.

"They pay me peanuts you know," she says, dragging on her fag.

We were sitting in the shed.

"It's slave labour. I've handed in my notice. Don't tell my Mum. She'd be furious."

I promised not to tell.

It was gruelling visiting Mum every few days. I often wondered what the benefits were of visiting when Mum would forget almost immediately that I'd been or even who I was. But according to the carers at the home, the feeling of companionship stayed with her throughout the day.

Visiting Dad is taking on similar levels of distress as his health fails and his need for care increases. Swallowing food has become a huge problem and with that comes the danger of choking so, we mash all his food, which is why I settled on shepherds pie, one of his favourite meals, for our Christmas lunch.

Lucy, Jenny and Ed had all, out of a sense of duty and sense of well placed loyalty, invited me over for Christmas Day. They didn't want me in the Spider House on my own. I didn't want me in the Spider House on my own either, but I also didn't want the fuss and bother of my children having to look after me. I told them I'd be spending the day with granddad and they could visit if they felt like it. No pressure.

Nicky is in a similar position, happily alone on Christmas Day and not wanting to be a burden on anyone, agreed to have lunch with Dad and visit Mum in the care home.

The care home was rammed to the rafters with residents, family members and loved ones, most of whom we'd never seen before, but there were a couple of regulars.

Like the husband who visited his wife who had early on set dementia. She was so young.

We find Mum waltzing along the corridor, draped in the gold and silver chains she'd pilfered from the Christmas Tree, wearing someone else's clothes. We sit together and have lunch. Chopping Dad's food, ducking Mum's food missiles and being jolly, along with everyone else. After lunch there is dancing. With residents and family already on the dance floor, Dad takes Mum's hand. They dance, peering into one another's eyes, like newly weds. It's utterly heart breaking but wonderful at the same time.

The care home is so busy with people coming and going that the three of us manage to slip out unnoticed. We arrive at Dad's flat, put the veg on, lay the table, complete with crackers, and make sure there's something suitably awful on the TV. As we sit there at the little wobbly dining table, wearing our paper hats, Nicky and I look at each other with a mixture of humour and incredible sadness.

Sadly no one visits. I don't blame them (Nicky does – with a vengeance). But who would want to stay sober enough to drive over to visit an old man who can't speak and then 'go on to' a dementia care home to sit with an old lady who, not only had no idea who they were but would quite possibly abuse them. Mum has a new habit of throwing cake or any other food lying around.

Dad didn't care about visitors, he was happy having us there. Maybe not as much as he loved his shepherds pie, four custard tarts (which he literally inhaled) and a big bowl of chocolates. Bizarrely it's one of the best Christmases I've ever had.

Twenty-Nine

My decision to start dating properly is an easy one. It isn't based on the desire to find 'the one' but a desire to do something (anything) to bring some excitement into my life. Even if that 'excitement' was enduring a (hopefully free) meal with an exceptionally dull man. It's also to stop the kids from worrying though I think Jenny, ever the worrier, is anxious that I'll be kidnapped, stabbed or just abused in some way.

The idea of having any kind of romantic liaison with someone working at the hospital is not only inadvisable but unprofessional and tacky. To be honest, it hadn't ever crossed my mind. I have witnessed dozens of affairs flourish and then fizzle out, sometimes with disastrous consequences; leading to messy, acrimonious divorces and broken hearts.

So that evening, I slalom my way through whatever row Fiona and her son are having when I step through the front door, and race upstairs to my room, hoping that the smell of fish and chips goes undetected. Fiona detests any kind of fried food. She says it reminds her of her Scottish ex-husband who liked to batter anything and everything. By 'batter' I mean the flour, egg and milk mixture, not assault and battery.

I sit on the loo in my bathroom, fish and chips unwrapped in the sink, laptop balanced on my knees. (I'm not peeing. I do have *some* standards you know) and log onto the dating website. I scan the faces and profiles of the ones that have clicked 'Favourite' on my profile. This is such a meat market. Maybe I could sort them in order of meat type: Pork chops, steaks, off-cuts, lamb, offal, sausage.

Fidel Castro:

"What's the most exciting thing you've done with a cigar?"

DELETE

manlybeard:

RUDE CHAT. DELETE.

Laidback:

SMUTTY. DELETE.

Searching4U

BORING. DELETE.

'young@heart'

FUNNY. FAVOURITE

Sunsets&wine

NEEDY. DELETE

'enereythe8th'

FRIENDLY. FAVOURITE

Yorkshire man1949

NICE. FAVOURITE

I delete the profiles that hint at bitterness:

Hurtb4:

"Looking for someone who won't walk out after 3 months."

Or made direct sexual references:

"What side of the bed do you like to sleep on?" and *"I'm good with my hands."*

Or used a sport in their profile name:

Live2Cricket / football / rugby / ski / shoot animals

Most want to be sure I am financially solvent (LOL):

"Must be financially solvent" or *"Career woman only"* or *"Must know what an ISA is"*

Some are downright unfriendly and make me wonder if they want a date or a lesson in armed combat.

Takeitorleaveit:

"I've had enough of drama queens."

A message from 'young@heart' He's keen. Or bored. Or a serial killer.

"I'm ironing. Please tell me you're doing something way more exciting?"

Lizzie123:

"I'm sitting on the loo eating fish and chips"

young@heart:

"Classy!"

Lizzie123:

"I'm very good at multi-tasking."

Silence. For ages. And ages.

I re-read my last message. *"I'm very good at multi-tasking"* Shit. That could be taken in any number of ways.

He thinks I'm a slut. I've blown it. Or maybe he's focussing on ironing the collar of his shirt.

Lizzie123:

"I didn't mean that in a rude way!"

My finger hovers over the 'send' button. What am I doing? Why am I worrying about what some invisible unknown desperate bastard, possible serial killer, thinks about me? I press delete.

young@heart:

"I can barely speak and walk at the same time!"

Phew. He has a sense of humour.

young@heart:

"Here's my email address. Let me know If you'd like to meet for a coffee."

Lizzie123:

"Or dinner?"

Again, I hover over the 'send' button.

Lucy's instructions tumble through my mind. I think about calling her. I can't keep running to my children every time I decide to do something. Anyway, I know what to do; meet in a safe place, straight after work, not too far from home. I'll have excuses ready – family dramas, seeing Mum, seeing Dad. Thinking about it none of them are excuses. They are actual 'things'.

I press send.

Thirty

'young@heart' looked everyone one of the sixty years in his photo. The 'interests' he listed on his profile were safe; theatre, galleries, walking, beach blah, blah and blah. I wasn't ready for anyone adventurous or demanding. I wanted to start with vanilla and work my way up to… I don't know, something with raisins in maybe.

The French restaurant was smart, warm, friendly and reassuringly busy. I didn't have time to do anything with my face before I left work, so he (and everyone else) was going to have to put up with my au naturel (read 'knackered') face. I am wearing a new dress that I'd bought in the sales (rugby tackling four other women to get my hands on it. At 70% discount, needs must.) and, yes, I have polished my shoes.

A lovely young waiter shows me to my table, pours me a glass of water and asks if I'd like a drink. I order a white wine.

I check my phone. I'm not early. He is late. Admittedly only seven minutes, if he turns up now, which he does. In his expensive suit and shoes, smelling (without wanting to go all Mills and Boon) of something deliciously musky.

"Well, this is a great first impression for you!" He kisses me on the cheek, as if we've known each other for years.

"I shan't insult you by apologising! I put my hands up to being crap at time keeping!" He's put me at ease and made me laugh within the space of a minute. "You look lovely!" he adds. I think I like this man.

"Right, I'm starving. I think we should throw caution to the wind and start with champagne and oysters! What do you reckon?" He's assertive without being controlling. I agree that oysters and champagne are a great idea.

He insists I order the most expensive steak on the menu. I don't argue. I also don't tell him it will be the first bit of joined up meat I've eaten in months.

The lovely waiter is diligent with the wine glass filling and, before I know it, we've finished bottle number two, sharing a pudding (something lemony) and ordering coffees.

While we wait for the coffees he nips to the gents, giving me a chance to concentrate my mind and consider my next move. Half of me, okay, the bigger half, which isn't a half, more like two thirds, wants to go on somewhere with him. His home perhaps. Or a hotel. But that was out of the question. I like him, but I don't know him.

'Going on' wasn't an option and neither was taking him 'back to mine'. Firstly, it wasn't 'mine' and secondly my bikini line resembles Epping Forest. I could kiss him though. That's acceptable, isn't it? What if he doesn't want to kiss me? What if he does that 'Well, lovely meeting you,

I hope you find someone.' brush off? I felt a spark. In fact, I reckon I had more sparks in my pants than in the entire National Grid.

'Going on', 'back to mine'… exciting new phrases I was keen to get used to. But not this evening.

The lovely waiter respectfully places the bill on the table. He tops my wine glass up with what's left in the bottle and clears the table of our empty dessert plates.

I finish my coffee and worry that 'young@heart's' coffee is going cold. I hope he's alright. I check my phone. It's nine o'clock. Excellent. I will be in bed by ten. A lovely evening followed by a good night's sleep.

"Would you like another coffee, Madam?" asks the lovely waiter.

"No, thank you. But, I wonder, would you mind checking the gent's toilets for me? My friend's been in there quite a while. I'm worried he might be ill." The waiter's nostrils flare alarmingly. "Not from the food! Just, you know, heart attack or something." The nostrils deflate. Clearly a heart attack is preferable to food poisoning.

"Of course, Madam."

As the waiter passes by the bar, he says something to the staff gathered around the till, they all turn to look at me. Do they know something I don't? Has he told them I've hinted at food poisoning? I didn't. He did. I rub my stomach in an overtly 'YUMMY FOOD' kind of way, just to be sure.

The waiter returns from the gents. "No gentleman in the toilets, Madam."

It takes me a while to register the full implications of this. The waiter, on the other hand, grasped the situation as soon as he'd stepped into the gents. 'young@heart' had done a runner. I've never wished a heart attack on anyone. Ever. I did now.

"Arsehole!"

"Would Madam like to come with me to the bar?"

I allow myself to be led to the bar, where the waiter physically manhandles me onto a stool and hands me a large brandy. I down it in one. Choke. Tear up. The lovely waiter hands me a napkin.

"I am sorry for your predicament, Madam."

"That's okay. The steak was lovely, by the way."

"Merci, Madam."

Mercy. I could do with some of that right now.

I blow my nose and hand him the sodden napkin back. More nostril flaring.

"I don't have my credit card with me. Would you mind waiting while I make a call?"

The waiter nods, understanding.

My 'mercy' arrives two hours later in the form of Lucy, dressed as Wonder Woman. She finds me at slumped at the bar, quite drunk, thanks to the three double brandies on top of the wine.

"Oh, Lucy. Sorry. I feel so stupid!"

I notice her outfit.

"Were you busy?"

"Yes. I was saving the world, but don't worry, I'm here now."

"Oh, no. You're angry with me. Are you angry with me?"

Yes. She is angry with me. She tells me off for not telling her I was going on a date. Then I get angry.

"Stop trying to control me!" then I sob for forgiveness and curse brandy and all types of wine.

Trying to hail a cab dressed as Wonder Woman with a drunken, sobbing woman beside you isn't easy, but Lucy manages it. I promise the driver that I won't vomit until I get home.

Lucy escorts me up the stairs and, after I've vomited in the loo, she puts me to bed.

"There's a dog down a well that needs rescuing. You going to be okay?" she says, as she tucks me in. I nod. I'll be fine. I'm going to find 'young@heart' and throw him down a well.

The next day I send 'young@heart' a message:

"Thank you for a wonderful evening. Sorry you had to leave so unexpectedly. I hope to see you again soon. I really think we connected really well." I was hoping he'd assume I paid the bill and didn't mind, because I was so steaming rich. I was hoping he'd be up for another date. I was hoping to bring Ed along. Smiley face.

Thirty-One

Fortunately, I didn't have time to dwell because I'd arranged to meet my next date, 'enereythe8th, the following day at a small Italian restaurant. It was a family run place, with tiny tables and shouty waiters. Too intimate for my liking but at least the food was cheap enough for me to pay should "enerythe8th" do a runner.

My plan to arrive early enough to scope out the gent's toilets and any possible escape routes are dashed when the waiter shows me to my table, where 'enerey and another woman are already waiting.

"Drink?" the waiter bellowed, before I even sat down.

"House white!' I screamed.

"Hello, I'm Cathy, John's ex-wife! Bet you weren't expecting that!" I can't help but notice that Cathy and I look creepily similar.

I shake her by the hand and look at John, who I didn't know was called John. I'd expected him to be called Henry.

"Oh, no. He just likes that song. *I'm 'Enerey the Eighth, I am, 'Enerey the Eighth I am, I am! I got married to the widow next door, She's been married seven times before"* Cathy brings all conversation and shouting in the entire restaurant to a staggering halt.

John nods, yes, he does like that song.

My wine arrives. I down it in one.

"No need to look at the menu. I've ordered us a sharing platter." What is it about dates and sharing platters.

Oh, John, you poor bastard.

"It was me who answered your message on the dating site. Don't get me wrong, I'm not some kind of control freak. He did ask me to." She laughs, I smile, John nods. I wonder if I'm being groomed for something.

To be fair (well done shouty Italian cook) the sharing platter was delicious. I ate most of it thanks to John being too intimidated to move and Cathy too busy firing questions at me; What was my background? My education? Why was I single? Did I have children? What was my financial status? And, my favourite, what was I looking for in a man?'

It was like a job interview, but for a job I didn't want. As soon as the sharing platter was cleared away I feigned receiving a text message.

"Oh! Time to go! Got to give my Dad his blanket bath!"

I added some sordid details involving adult nappies and commode; just to stop Cathy's jaw flapping. My offer of 'going Dutch' was declined and I legged it out of the restaurant.

I sent a message to 'enereythe8th' the next day

"Thanks for the lovely meal, Cathy. I'm sure John will find someone soon enough. If you'll let him."

I check the dating site for new 'likes' and notice that Yorkshireman still hasn't responded to my 'like'. That's just rude. Maybe he can't see from under his flat cap. Maybe his whippet is preventing him from going on line.

Thirty-Two

The bad vibes at Spider's Nest have grown from uncomfortable to unbearable. Without so much as a 'hello' or 'goodbye' passing between Fiona and me any more I'm starting to have flashbacks to my childhood; if the radio was on in the kitchen when I got back from school then all was well. I could chat with mum about all the things I'd done that day. But coming home to silence meant going straight to your room and supper eaten in stomach churning silence. This would last for hours, days or weeks. Then, as quickly as it started, it ended. As if nothing had happened. I was a nervous wreck during the summer holidays.

I dream about moving out the way some people dream about having a yacht; unattainable unless you win the lottery or rob a bank. I've gone over my finances time and time again, ever hopeful that the bank would inadvertently deposit rather than withdraw.

I grab at the chance of organising a family lunch at the house, safe in the knowledge that Fiona and her son are trying to kill themselves on the snowy slopes of an Austrian mountain. Skiing and arguing at great expense.

I've splashed the cash on a joint of lamb with all the trimmings, Lucy, Jenny , boyfriend and Ed's favourite. It's like old times. The family sitting around the dining table enjoying Sunday lunch. I wish I could do this in my own home, not some spider loving woman's house.

Jenny lightly squeezes my hand "You'll have your own place one day. Don't worry." That sets me off.

"How? When? When I've paid off my debts? When's that going to happen? Never! I'm going to be stuck here till I die!" I whine, cranking up the self-pity to factor 11.

"Rubbish. You'll just have to be a bit more savvy." Lucy says. "What's the rent on this place?"

"Six hundred and fifty pounds."

"What costs do you have that you can get rid of?"

"None".

"How much is it costing to store your shit?" asks Ed, going for the popular 'get rid' consensus.

"One hundred and seventy five pounds" I whimper.

"A month?" Ed's shocked that an empty 'room' can generate so much money when used for storing other people's 'shit'.

"No, silly. A week."

Ed practically falls off his chair. "Are you mental?"

"No, Ed, thank you. I'm not mental. That's what it costs. I've got a lot of stuff. And no, I'm not getting rid of it."

I know most people would have sold their 'shit' the moment the shit hit the fan, but I couldn't. I wasn't ready to dispose of thirty five years-worth of life for a few quid. I've downsized, cut back and whittled my life to the bone. Selling my 'shit' would be a defeat. I've done defeat. I want to do 'winning'.

"What if you downsize…" cautious Jenny dares to suggest.

"NO!"

"…and put the stuff…"

"Shut up all of you. I'm not parting with it!"

"… in our garage? There's plenty of space. Or will be once we sort our stuff out." Jenny looks at her boyfriend who has no choice but to agree.

Lucy calculates "That way you'll have about seven hundred pounds a month to play with. Which, if you're careful, means you can look from somewhere to rent around the eleven hundred pounds mark. A studio flat maybe."

Surely a yacht is just around the corner then?

In the kitchen, everyone watches me scrub away every trace of having cooked a meal.

"Feel free to join in!" I say. "Don't hold back on my account."

Ed pours everyone more wine. That's his way of helping.

"So, what's the latest on the dating front?" Lucy asks. I can tell she's reported my bad experience with young@ heart when four pairs of concerned eyes swivel in my direction.

"Nothing to report," I lie "Not sure I can be bothered with any of them."

"Oh, come on! You can't let one bad apple spoil your barrel," Jenny says. Ed retches at the thought of his mother having a sex life.

"It's my barrel; I'll do what I like with it!" I reply. Ed retches again.

"Let's have a look at them!" Jenny says "I bet there are some real dogs on there."

"I bet Pa's on there! God! Imagine if you responded accidentally and ended up going on a date and it was him!" All three of them have a laugh at my expense.

"Have any of you bothered to visit Nanny or Granddad recently?"

A resounding silence.

Ha! Touché.

Thirty-Three

I aim for a minimum of two or three dates a week. Determined to build up my confidence and, if nothing else, have a proper meal. I know, I know. In this day and age of equality and feminism I should be offering to pay my way but sod that. I am skint. And, with all the toing and froing with Mum and Dad I'm not feeling at all guilty.

LAIDBACKGUY59 82%

Profile : 59, 6 foot tall. Eyes of blue. Interests –

Why lie about your age on a dating profile? Or, for that matter, your height. Unless you intend to remain sitting in a darkened room, there isn't any point.

We meet at a very expensive restaurant. No way is Lucy going to be able to cover this bill if he does a runner. Champagne is already on ice when I arrive. Delicious starter followed by sumptuous main.

For once I'm dining with a 'listener', to the point of his saying absolutely nothing. I wonder if he might be deaf; his facial expression doesn't change and he cocks his head to one side, like a bird. I test him with a question.

"Do you have any children?"

AND THEN IT HAPPENED.

With a fork full of roast duck half way to his mouth he leans across the table and licks, yes LICKS, the left side of my face. Not just a little "you taste good" sort of a lick but a "Boy, this ice lolly is worth savouring" kind of a lick. I freeze. Shocked. I mean, what do you do? Carry on talking? Carry on eating? Punch him in the face?

"I'm so sorry," he says. "I just couldn't help myself. You have such wonderful skin."

I smile politely. Finish my lemon sole in silence and, as the table is cleared, excuse myself. I head for ladies. As soon as I'm out of sight I head towards the cloakroom.

"You're the third one he's brought here this week" says the cloakroom lady, as she hands me my coat. "Probably best if you leave through the back door. He won't see you then."

I sneak out, disappointed not to have made it to pudding.

'BLINDDATE'

OK, that's not a profile name. I am on an actual blind date courtesy of a work colleague who can't get her head around the fact that I am still single. I have tried to reassure her that I am happy being on my own but she won't have it.

So, here I am, at a black-tie event sitting next to a recently divorced 'normal' man. He's the right height and even the right age, but man alive, he's dull. I am genuinely contemplating falling on my knife and fork for the sake of my sanity. It's that or sticking said knife and fork in his thigh.

He will not stop going on about his children's school fees, his pension, his love of ordnance survey maps.

After the main course, I excuse myself and head straight for the cloakroom, grab my coat and jump on a bus.

I wonder if I'll ever make it to pudding.

'CHARIOTOFFIRE' 78%

Profile: Blah...blah...blah.

I realise I've been to some lovely restaurants lately, at the expense of others. I've had some lovely food, thanks to the generosity of others. I'm slightly shocked that I feel a sense of disappointment when I arrive at the chain café for my next date. I know! Appalling of me to think that.

It's a big noisy, open plan place. I half expect the staff to burst into song while transporting a cake adorned with a Roman candle to a table of ten-year-olds. I know! I can't believe I thought that either.

I spot my date chatting on his mobile, sitting at a table near the toilets. This is awkward. I rely on 'popping to the ladies' as part of my get-out plan. That's going to be impossible here. But who knows? Maybe I won't need to escape this time.

I approach, smiling, make eye contact. He holds up a finger 'hold on' while he finishes his call. Okay, could be important. Could be bad timing. Could be one of his kids. I'll give him the benefit of the doubt. I sit and pour myself a glass of water.

"Yes, I promise. Of course. Yes… Yes… Yes… Yes… Bye." He turns to me and I know *immediately* he's disappointed.

More often than not these dates are not going to have a spark. It's hit and miss. That's part of the fun. But that face, that expression, he could have tried harder not to look like a petulant child.

"Hi, I'm Lizzie."

"Sorry about that!" He says, not bothering to make eye contact.

"I've just had another bloody child. Mother's only twenty. Met her skiing last year. That's the 'thing' with men. We can carry on spreading our seed!" He beams, so proud of himself.

Forget pudding, I'm not sure I'm going to hang around for starters.

But I do; I eat my starter in silence, while he talks about himself. I interject once or twice, my polite default setting kicks in. As the table is cleared for the next course I lay a twenty pound note on the table.

"I think that covers everything I've had."

"Where are you going? We haven't even ordered the main yet. It's a bit rude to just leave half way through, don't you think?"

I'm pleased he looks embarrassed AND finally making eyeball contact.

"Okay," I say "If you can answer three questions I'll stay."

He frowns. Clearly not used to having any demands for his attention put on him.

"What's my name? How many children do I have? Where do I live?"

He laughs. Arrogant twat.

"I don't know… Laurie? Lorna? Two. three offspring? Something… Park? Seriously, what's that got to do anything?"

I leave. No main course and no bloody pudding!

'COUNTRYWALKS' 86%

Finally. Nice looking. Good suit. The 'right' shoes. Even, praise be, the right height.

I enter the restaurant and see him sitting at the bar, glass of chilled rosé in his hand, chatting amiably with the barman.

I should have known something was amiss there and then. His eyes, lovely as they were in repose, a sexy green/ blue, are swivelling round the room like ball bearings. Maybe he was a spy. Maybe he had dry eye syndrome.

He stood as I approached. Good manners and a lovely smile. We introduced ourselves and were shown to a table by an attentive waiter. Another glass and a fresh bottle of rosé was brought to the table. Maybe he'd already had a bottle and hence the continuing eye swivel. Maybe he's just nervous. We both are to be honest.

I break the ice with "Have you come far?" Despite sounding like the Queen it's always a good start.

Before he could answer a woman joins us at our table. She's joined by a guy. I look around, there are plenty of empty tables.

"Excuse me, but there are other tables available."

Neither of them move; I'm about to up the ante on the 'can you just go away?', front when the guy starts taking photos of me and my date on his phone, making sure to get both of us in the same shot. I suddenly wonder if my date is famous and find myself leaning in. How can I not know which side of my face is the good one? I smile, I can't help myself.

There's so much chaos around me that it takes a while for me to understand what's going on. The other woman is his wife and I was, in fact, the 'other woman'. She had him. Bang to rights. Even though there had been no banging. I must say, I was impressed with her initiative. I left them to it but not before suggesting that she might like to check out his dating site history before photographing other women without their consent.

When I got home I stood before the mirror and worked out which side of my face was the better side. Left.

Thirty-Four

I pick Mum up from the care home in a taxi. Getting the Battered Bitch was too much of a faff. Taking the bus to Lucy's, driving to the care home, then back to Lucy's then the bus. No. Not today. Today is all about taking the easy route.

Nicky's taken Dad to one of the many funerals he insists on attending. We keep pointing out to him that the more funerals he attends the fewer people will attend his but he has a strong sense of loyalty and it gets him out and socialising.

It's cold. Too cold to go for a long walk in the park, which is something Mum loves; walking and chatting to anyone that comes along, stealing other people's dogs, picking flowers she shouldn't pick and generally having a whale of a time, leaving me to clear up dog kidnap accusations and threats of court action from park keepers. It's still difficult coaxing Mum out of the car and into the home, but her dementia has advanced to a stage where she's more childlike and less aggressive.

"We're going to Jenny's."

"Who's Jenny?"

"She's a friend. You'll like her."

"No I won't."

Mum doesn't like 'friends'. I've given up reminding her that Jenny or Lucy or Ed is her grandchild. They are now friends that she quickly forgets.

"We're going to help her sort out her garage."

"Why can't she sort her own bloody garage? Hasn't she got any arms?"

I manage not to laugh again at her swearing.

I've given the requisite one month's notice to the storage people and worked out that if I put the money spent on the storage aside for two or three months I should have enough for a deposit on a flat. Maybe the light at the end of the tunnel isn't a train after all.

Jenny's garage is full of bikes, canoes and boxes (and boxes) of 'stuff'. While Jenny and I throw things in bin bags Mum fills her four handbags with anything she fancies.

After an hour, we retire to the kitchen to prepare lunch. Mum is given the ribbon box to sort through. The ribbon box is a lifesaver. It keeps Mum busy for a good hour while she chats utter nonsense.

"Is Dad picking me up from school today?" she asks, while winding a long blue ribbon around a bottle of HP sauce.

"I don't know. Would you like him to?" I ask, happy to go along with whatever world she's in.

Mum shrugs. "He's always late."

"I'll make sure he's on time," I say.

Mum moves on from the HP bottle and lays lengths of ribbon out on the table. "Is Dad picking me up?"

"Yes. I think so."

And so, it goes on for the entire lunch. Jenny and I talk while, at the same time, responding to Mum's 'other world' conversation.

After lunch I give Nicky a call while Jenny gets ready for a job interview she has lined up.

"Nicky. It's Lizzie. Just checking you haven't forgotten you're picking Mum up from Jenny's later. Hope the funeral was fun."

"I've got to go, I can't be late." Jenny, dressed to impress, hovers in the doorway.

'Go! Go! Nicky's probably on her way. Or her phone battery's flat."

"Cool. Everything's laid out on the bed. Take your pick!"

Mum and I wave Jenny off.

"When is my dad coming?" Mum asks. She's tired and fractious. She wants to 'go home'.

"Soon," I say, praying for a 'dad' to magically appear and take her away.

I get the duvet and pillows from the spare room and make up a bed for Mum on the sofa. If she's a 'child' then she can have a nap! Mum snuggles down while I tell her a story. She's out like a light. Peace and quiet.

My phone rings.

"Liz, it's me. I'm on the M3 with Dad."

"What are you doing there?"

"What do you think I'm doing here? Having a fucking picnic! Dad's bloody car broke down!" Nicky's clearly having a very stressful day.

"Oh, N~o~o~o~o!"

"I'm not going to be able to pick Mum up. Will you be able to get her back okay"

"Yes. How's Dad?"

"Cold and hungry. If the AA don't arrive soon I'm going to flash my tits at the next passing lorry and commandeer the vehicle!"

Nicky hangs up. I look down at Mum, fast asleep. I'll order a taxi to take us back to the home when she wakes up.

I call the care home.

"Hi, it's Lizzie. I've still got Mum. Just so you don't think I've kidnapped her. She's asleep. I'll bring her back later. Is that all right?"

No. No, it isn't. They don't want her back half way through tea time. It would upset the rest of the residents. With their hands full at feeding time, the last thing the carers want to have to deal with is Mum kicking off. I have to bring her back afterwards. In four hours' time.

Confession. I don't have a meeting. I have a date. With 'Sunsets&Wine' aka George.

I have everything planned. For once I'm not rushing from work. For once I am going to take my time. We've spent weeks trying to arrange a date. I was going to have a long soak in the bath. Jenny was lending me something to wear. My poverty diet meant we were the same size. Lucy had offered her Wonder Woman outfit but I declined.

I was going to have to cancel. Bugger!

Me: Hi. I'm sorry but I have a problem with my Mum and will have to cancel.
George: Nothing serious I hope.
Me: No, not serious. Can't get her back to the home till later this evening.
George: Why not bring her along! What's the worst that can happen?!

Seriously? I love this man! But Mum, I can't just drag her to a strange place, full of strange people just to satisfy my needs, can I? She might freak out. Worse, she might throw a few punches. Worse still she might refuse to go at all.

Me: Really? She's quite mad, you know.
George: Aren't we all?
Me: Okay! On your head be it!

Mum woke up and, after a cup of tea and a slice of cake, was happy to let me brush her hair and polish her shoes. She even let me wash her face with a flannel.

"We're going on an adventure. We're going to meet a new friend!"

"Does Dad know?"

I shake my head, no. "It can be our secret" I realise that, as her 'Mum' I am confessing to meeting another man behind her 'Dad's' back. Honestly, things get very complicated when there's a whole other universe involved.

We arrive at the restaurant and find George waiting for us at a table set back from the main thoroughfare. He's pre-ordered a bottle of wine – three glasses.

"Blimey, you're a bit of all right aren't you," She says, as he holds out a chair for her.

Somewhere between Jenny's flat and this restaurant, Mum has slipped into East End mode. No longer a child, she's now racy and more than a bit outspoken.

"You're not so bad yourself." George has got the measure of Mum in all of five seconds.

I quickly pour water in Mum's wine glass but not quickly enough. She grabs my glass and takes a huge gulp while waving at the waiter.

"G and T please, love!"

"No!" I yell. "We're fine with just the wine thank you!"

"Shut yer face!" 'Old' Mum is definitely in the building and now working the room.

It's downhill from then on. For me. Mum and George, on the other hand, have a great time cracking jokes and flirting. Don't get me wrong, I loved seeing Mum so happy but I couldn't get a word in edgeways.

Any attempt I make at getting to know George or telling him about myself is cut short; by Mum telling me to shut my face.

I nearly wept with relief when Nicky arrived to take her back to the home.

"THAT SLUT! HAS STOLEN MY BOYFRIEND!" yelled Mum, pointing at me, as Nicky led her out of the restaurant to the taxi waiting outside. The date carries on but it isn't the same, we had to be grown up and 'normal'.

I got a text from Nicky when I got back home.

"Took me an hour to get Mum settled. Apparently, you made her have sex with some random bloke. Honestly, Lizzie, how could you? Lol."

I send her a 'thumbs up' too exhausted to write anything and not wanting to spoil the happy glow I felt after having a *proper* kiss and the promise of a second date from George.

Mum was right. He was a bit of all right.

Thirty-Five

Profile: Divorced after a long marriage and back in the UK having lived in Africa for 8 years. Financially solvent with a meaningful career. Looking for someone to be a long term companion and who doesn't mind my regular travels on business. Age correct and picture recent.

90%. Wowzers! The highest compatibility rating so far. But, judging by the few dates that I've been on, this isn't necessarily an accurate measure. I was more than a little sceptical.

I was so annoyed that I was popping up on Yorkshireman's page and being ignored, that I decided to flush him out. After plucking up enough courage (okay, after having had a glass of wine) I sent him a message.

"Hiya YM. We're 90% compatible which makes me wonder what the missing 10% is all about. Any thoughts?"

"*Animals ? I don't like animals.*"

"Rolling Stones or Beatles?"

"Rolling Stones."

"Theatre or Cinema?"

"Cinema. You?"

"Ah! There we have it. Opposite to all of the above!"

At work, during lunch or on my way to a meeting, I'd wing another question over and wait for the response.

We end up chatting on line about our work, life and anything else that popped up in the following couple of weeks until he eventually said "I suppose we had better meet." That made me laugh. Steady on, I thought, you'll burst a blood vessel at this rate. The passion! But then, he is from Yorkshire and they don't waste time on words.

I've given up twisting myself into impossible positions to wax and pluck various parts of my body. I didn't do it for public viewing, I did it for myself. But eventually that passed too.

I went to the pub after work with a few colleagues and then at seven o'clock jumped on a bus to the agreed meeting place, a lovely French restaurant. I was nervous, this restaurant was on 'my patch'. I'd visited it many times with colleagues and clients.

All previous dates had been nearer to Spider house than work so that I could get home easily. If he turned out to be five foot four and eighty years old I didn't want anyone from work strolling in and witnessing the encounter. He was also one of the few men online that I'd really wanted to meet. Then it had taken so long to get a response and then a date, I was a nervous wreck. I had a terrible feeling, in the pit of my stomach that this was going to go terribly wrong.

I spotted him at the bar with a glass in one hand and a bottle in the other. He has a kind (but sad) face, lovely silver hair and (praise be!) was the right height.

"Glass or bottle?" he asks.

"Bottle," I say.

The bottle became supper, then another bottle and then… pudding! I talk, he listens. I find myself wanting to make him smile. He talks, eventually and I listen. His work is all consuming and he travels a lot. I agree to another date. I want to jump up and down saying, "When? When? When?"

Instead I nod, yeah, sure. Play it cool, Lizzie, play it cool.

Annoyingly I can't get Yorkshireman out of my head. I send him a few messages after our date, thanking him for a lovely evening but get zero response. Obviously, I take this lack of response personally. After a few more (unhinged) messages he eventually responds. Turns out he hates chatter for the sake of it. That's new for a chatterbox like me. Biting my fist is the only way to stop myself sending any more messages.

Fortunately, the next date was only a week away.

I'd pulled out all the stops too. New dress. New hair. Old underwear. Well, let's not go overboard.

We meet up in a lovely little restaurant, still on 'my patch' but not minding who saw us.

As we made our way over to our table, G and T's in hand, I gave him a surreptitious once over; yes, he was still 'hot'. We sat and quietly perused our menus.

"I've been giving our last meeting some thought," he said, without looking up from the wine list.

"Oh, yes?" I said. A marriage proposal? So soon? Why, Mr. Darcy!

"Romance is definitely not on the cards."

Why Mr. Darcy, you utter shit.

"I feel I ought to air my concerns before we go any further." He sounded like a bank manager and I was being denied an overdraft.

Being a Yorkshire man through and through he was worried that I a) had no money, b) was too posh and c) my children were clearly my world and would come first in any relationship. 'Too posh'? The last time I'd heard that was from my bullying 'rock holding' boss'; she was a Northerner too.

"I could have lied to you about the money and, of course, my children are important to me and would always come first. It's called being a mother. I thought you liked honesty?"

Unlike others, Yorkshireman didn't have a profile picture on the dating site that was ten years old. It was a recent one, taken by someone he'd dated, that's how painfully honest he was. He was honest about his height, where others so often weren't. He was exactly as he had described himself. And that's how I wanted him to be.

The discussion during dinner was animated, to say the least. To be honest I was surprised the dinner didn't end sooner but there was no denying, for me anyway, that we had a connection and not even our 'first row' terminated the evening.

We ended up saying farewell at the bus stop and even had a very lovely kiss. But I went back to Spider House with a sense of foreboding; wondering if I'd ever see him again.

One of the things I wanted, more than a man (at the time) was to see my children getting on with their own lives and not continually worrying about me. Sometimes I tell a small lie, pretending I'm busy when in fact I'm watching TV in my room which, to be honest, was one of my favourite pastimes.

I'm almost a year into internet dating and feeling good about myself. I have a new-found confidence, I know I'll be all right, come what may. I'm not saying I'm out of the woods, I need to get out of this house before I start feeling anything like that, but, as the doctor advised, I've stopped focusing on the trees.

Thirty-Six

Nicky and I were resigned to another Christmas at the care home and shepherd's pie with Dad but New Year was looming and Lucy, Jenny and Ed had all dropped hints that they'd 'include me'. Nothing appealed to me less than being the oldest swinger in town at some 'event' or other so I take a leap of faith with Charles, aka 'mykindoftown'.

I had gone out with Charles a few times and although I didn't think we really clicked, I thought he was fun. I knew he wanted to take things further but I didn't. It was nice to be courted though.

One evening, when he picked me up for dinner, Fiona introduced herself. I knew what her game was, flirting and emphasising he was in *her* house. I wasn't fussed. I've never been a jealous type.

But the next day, when I was on my way out, she asked me for his number.

"I think I'd get on better with him than you as he's quite an intelligent man."

I decided then and there, to give myself a month to find a flat and move out. I handed over his number and suggested we arrange diaries, to prevent double bookings.

When Charles suggested that we spend New Year's long weekend in Paris I leapt at the chance. I love that city and hadn't been for a very long time. Even more enjoyable was telling Fiona.

Jenny insisted on driving us to the airport. I knew she wasn't doing this purely out of the kindness of her heart but to suss my date out. She didn't like him and told me so when he was in the gents.

"He's after one thing and one thing only! You can do a lot better. *And* he's shorter than you!"

"Yes, I'm sure I can do better, but right now I'm just going to Paris with a friend, okay? And as for him being after 'one thing', what do you think I'm after?" That's not strictly true; I wasn't after anything other than a nice time and being in Paris. But I wasn't going to be dictated to by one of my children.

After waving (a slightly sulky) Jenny off, Charles and I headed to Departures. He asked for my passport which I handed over without a second thought.

It wasn't till we were on the other side that I felt a chill run down my spine. Taking my passport from me was a very 'William' thing to do; he used to make fun of me not being able to do 'grown-up things like look after tickets, passports, documents, that kind of thing. Controlling. Maybe I am being paranoid. Maybe he's just being helpful. Maybe I'll just ask for my passport back.

"Why?" he asks

"Because it's mine!" I snap. Then, just to soften it "And I want to shop!" I have no idea why I felt the need to soften the blow.

Charles reluctantly hands me my passport. Oh, God. Please don't let him be a William Mark II. I don't have any romantic inclinations towards him but I am hoping for a fun time in a beautiful city and if he's William Mark II I might end up killing him. Or myself. No, definitely him.

During the flight, he regales me with tales of his awful, money grabbing (sensible) wife. She drank too much. Especially red wine. He found the red staining of her teeth repulsive. She ate too much, especially chicken. What's wrong with chicken? He tells me, in great detail, how battery chickens are farmed. okay. Maybe I'll stop eating chicken.

Bringing in the New Year dressed as a Bavarian beer maid at one of Lucy's events was suddenly looking preferable. I wonder if I could get the pilot to turn the plane round.

As soon as we land, Charles is on his mobile, shouting obscenities at some poor woman in his office. Even the taxi driver is appalled, and he's French.

We arrive at the hotel, a beautiful old place right in the middle of St. Germain and are shown to our room, complete with a spectacular view of the Eiffel Tower.

Charles leaves the bathroom door open while he pees loudly and continues to shout at the woman on the other end of his mobile. There's no way she can't hear him peeing. What a squalid little man!

I start to unpack.

Before I'm even half unpacked Charles exits the bathroom, stripped down to his boxers. He's still on his phone but gives me a 'look' to indicate a) he won't be a minute and b) we're going to have sex.

The sight of him, with his pot belly and tight underpants makes me shudder, and not in a good way.

"Let's not rush. We're here for the whole weekend. Let's go for a wander," I say, as soon as he's off the phone, praying that the flirty 'you wait till I get you back' tone pays off.

I walk him around the streets of Paris as if he were an over tired four year old. I coo and ooh at the sexy lingerie in the shop windows. For a while he looks hopeful but after the fifth shop window his hopes were, thankfully, fading. He could barely stand by the time we found a lovely little restaurant down a beautiful, quiet street. I had no idea where we were. I didn't really care, as long as we weren't in our hotel room.

"Waiter! More wine!" I do that, when he's away from the table, and practically neck it before he gets back. The waiter keeps my glass topped up whenever Charles' head is turned. Over supper he reminds me that drinking to excess is very unattractive in a woman. If only I hadn't given him my passport. If only I'd stayed at home.

I 'accidentally' order chicken and insist he doesn't send it back. I promise to brush my teeth before bed but draw the line at the suggested full-on purge. The man's insane.

We're both pretty drunk by the time we leave the restaurant. The waiter gives us a surly nod as we crash out of the door.

Neither Charles nor I know where we are and it takes us a good two hours to find our way back to the hotel. Note to self; Parisians are not the most helpful people when it comes to giving direction, but then we were violently swaying while speaking O level French.

By the time we get back to the hotel I worry that Charles may have sobered up enough to attempt a second offensive and I worry that I may only have my garlic breath to rely on as a defence.

We stagger up to our room and both of us collapse onto the bed. Charles is out like a light and I'm not far behind. Phew.

I had the most wonderful dream. I was walking along a beach with diamond white sand, the cloudless sky a brilliant blue. Not a soul in sight. The sand oozes between my toes as the turquoise sea laps over my feet.

I'm woken by a sound and a sensation I can't work out. Maybe it's my brain sloshing around in my head. Maybe there are rats in the room, nibbling at the marvellous panelling. My head is in the room but my feet are still in the oozing sand.

I lift my head and look down at my feet. I would have preferred to see a rat chewing at the bloody stumps of my legs rather than Charles sucking my toes. There he was, sitting on a chair, facing the bed, foot in hand (mine, not his), sucking away on my toes. Some might find the dribbling and sucking sexy. Not me. I leap out of bed and accidentally (I swear) catch him in the face with my freshly sucked foot. He falls back off the chair on to the floor, blood streams down his face as he writhes around in agony.

"You've broken my nose!"

Desperate for a pee I leap out of bed, step over Charles and lock myself in the bathroom.

"We need to talk!" I shout above the noise of my peeing.

"Bitch!" he yells back at me.

Later, after the hotel doctor had attended to Charles' nose I apologise.

"I don't know what I was thinking. I like you but not in *that* way."

"Then why the hell did you agree to come along then?" Understandably he's disappointed.

"Because I thought we could have a lovely weekend as good friends. I didn't realise there were 'conditions.'"

"Well, we would have had a nice time if you weren't such a frigid cow! You can't see a good thing when it's staring you in the face. "

"Trust me, but *nothing* I've seen over the last twenty four hours has been 'good.'"

"I've turned down better women than you!"

"Oh, grow up! You need to learn to take no for an answer. You're just another short arsed old man. Deal with it."

"You wait. You'll be running back to me within the month!"

I'm packed and ready to leave within the hour and, with my passport and boarding pass in hand, I take a taxi to the airport. Three hours later I'm on a plane bound for London.

There is a positive side to all this. Returning home without anyone knowing means I can see in the New Year alone in my room. Yes, I could have pottered around art galleries, eaten a kebab while window shopping along the Kings Road or sat in the cinema watching a film I'd never confess to seeing, but I preferred home.

I tried to stay awake for Big Ben but was asleep by ten o'clock. I've never been a fan of New Year's Eve celebrations anyway. It's depressing: the empty promises, the false expectations, the kissing. No, I'd rather lounge around in my pyjamas, snacking and drinking tins of ready-made G and T.

Thirty-Seven

"You have to promise me that even if I'm in a coma, DO NOT leave hairs on my chin" as stated by Mum twenty odd years ago, when the first wiry hair appeared on her chin. "I'd rather die than end up looking like one of those bearded old ladies!" I promised. Nicky promised. We're both at that stage ourselves now. Neither of us leaves the house without at least two pairs of tweezers. The 'general tweezer' – for those easy bum fluff strays that appear in the middle of your neck and catch the light, and 'serious tweezer' – with the pointed end that could remove shrapnel (or, as I discovered, gouge a hole in your face), but in our case, cope with the hard, wiry little buggers on the chin.

Mum would sit like a child, seeming not to notice, chatting away or humming to herself as one of us plucked away at her wires. Satisfying for both parties and often preferable to a lot of the dates I went on. Was I enjoying sitting here with this man, sipping wine/coffee, or would I rather be listening to my mother's prattle, while plucking her chin? The chin won on quite a few occasions.

In between plucking Mum, feeding Dad, work, dating and living with a spider loving nutter, I look for a flat. First, I tried established estate agents.

"What are you looking for Mrs. Watkins?"

"*Large* studio or one bed. Preferably in south London. And, if possible, no more that £900 – £1000 all in."

I watch the estate agent diligently enter everything into his/her computer.

"And will you act as guarantor?"

"For who? It's for me."

And it was tits up from thereon in.

"Oh, I thought this was for... one of your..."

"Children? No. Just me."

"A London base?" He/she would say, with hope. The hope being that I wasn't as impoverished as they feared. Poverty is just, like, *so* embarrassing?

"No. My London home," I'd say, bright and cheery but wanting to slam his/her face into the computer.

Big nasal sigh from the estate agent as he/she digs in the computer equivalent of the bottom drawer for something that isn't 'boasting' of anything other than lack of dignity and sanitation.

I'm shown around some appalling places. I know what it's like to be desperate but seeing what's available, for that amount of money makes me furious. Landlords are taking the piss!

Then I try a less established estate agent. Just the one, with an office above a funeral parlour.

The estate agent is a nice Indian man who, discovering I was single, decided to show me something just around the corner.

"Easy for shopping, work, eating out," he said.

This sounds promising, I thought, until I discovered it was above a take-away (that'll be the eating out bit then). It was a large multi-occupancy six bedroom dwelling. It could have been a glorious flat if I had no sense of smell, but now it was a multi-occupancy. Each room had a lock on it. Behind the locked door was a bedsit. As he showed me round, young people stepped out of their rooms to say hello. Eastern European, Chinese, French, Arabic, all smiling and saying 'Hi'. He showed me the communal kitchen, each cupboard numbered to its corresponding room. I'm too old for this.

"Gas oven!" said the estate agent, proudly.

"Is it big enough for my head" I wondered. Maybe I could do a deal with the funeral parlour downstairs. God, this is too depressing.

I constantly check the property section in the local papers, taking into account that 'local' is one of the most expensive areas in London, I don't find anything under fifteen hundred pounds that isn't a glorified cupboard with hot and cold running mould.

And then, just when I'd started to contemplate living in a box under Wandsworth Bridge, I hear that Charlotte, a trusted work colleague, is moving out of her flat in Richmond. Yes, Richmond. Not just one of *London's* most expensive Boroughs but one of the *country's* most expensive Boroughs. Reach for the stars! Because that's worked so well up to now, hasn't it?

Charlotte's getting married and setting up home with her future spouse in a month's time. I call her landlord, already primed by Charlotte, and we set up a meeting at the flat.

"But, what if he doesn't like me?" I whine, "What if my financial 'situation' is a problem?" I keep that in my head. No need for anyone to hear about that gory business.

"Of course, he'll like you. And if you don't get this flat then he probably has other ones in the same area."

The flat is in a huge house near the top of Richmond Hill. One of two 'multi-occupancy' houses in a street of seven million pound houses with cars parked out front that cost more than most people earn in a year.

I fell in love with it before I was even through the door. Because it had a door. With a lock. It had a kitchen, bedroom, sitting room and bathroom; separated by actual walls. As I savoured the sensation of walking from one room to another the landlord asked me how I had managed to get myself into the predicament of being a lady of a certain age without property.

I gave him the highlights, like a film trailer – William's soul mate, mortgage, financial destitution, Lucy's flat, my job and current residence at spider ranch.

He suggested, once he'd prised me unwillingly out of the flat, to make him an offer. For a second I thought he was suggesting 'favours' but that passed when I looked at his kind, concerned face. No sign of his wanting to whisk me off to Paris, thank God.

That evening I sent him an email. My offer was short of his asking price and would have to cover everything except the Council Tax. I said that, if he let me move in, he would never have to worry about me or the property. I would treat it as my own. Clean the stairwell, look out for others living in the house and weed the front garden/ parking area.

I convinced myself he would say no. I fell so short of the asking price, it made no sense for him to say yes. While I waited for a response I calculated and re-calculated my outgoings.

If I paid the same rent as Charlotte, on top of my debt payments and even without the storage fees, I wouldn't have enough to live on. I wouldn't even be able to get to work, let alone eat. I decide to call him the next day and say thank you, but no thank you. I couldn't take the financial strain.

A minute later an email arrives in my inbox from the landlord. I have absolutely no idea why but he's said yes! I shall go to the Ball! I conga around my bedroom. Charlotte, Charlotte. You Rock! Charlotte, Charlotte, You Rock!

"I have got a front *DOOR!* I have got a front *DOOR!* Ner, ner, ner, ner, *NER!*"

Thirty-Eight

Surprise, surprise, Yorkshireman gets in touch asking if I'd like to spend the following weekend with him. I was understandably excited at the prospect. 'Spending a weekend' meant only one thing, didn't it? Yes, it did. Rumpy of the pumpy.

The week dragged and gave me plenty of time to panic, pull myself together and then panic some more. When Saturday finally arrived I got to his flat stupidly early, just as he was coming back from shopping. My immediate dread, thanks to my week long fantasies of leaping in to bed as soon as we saw each other at the start of the 'spending the weekend' weekend was based on the probability of our now having sex in broad daylight, not the much needed (dim) candlelight. After three children, and various lumps and bumps I was uncomfortable with any form of close inspection.

He looked slightly taken aback at my early arrival and, sensing that I was a nervous wreck, suggested we go for a walk. A very, *very*, long walk on Hampstead Heath, interspersed with coffee breaks and window shopping in Hampstead itself.

Four hours later I was still a wreck, although pretending to be fine, as we headed back to his flat. Instead of watching the football match on television he so desperately wanted to, he now had to deal with this neurotic woman who wanted sex but didn't. We were both stone cold sober and feeling awkward.

Needless to say it wasn't great and we were both relieved when it was over. For him it must have been like trying to make love to an ironing board. I could see he was glad too. Nothing to do with the expression on his face, but just by the speed with which he switched on Sky Sports. But, hey! I was over my shag block! I should have left there and then with a "Thank you, and goodnight!" but I was hoping for a replay. The one with candlelight and alcohol.

I was doing quite a good impression of a satisfied female who just wanted to snooze for a good hour. I couldn't doze, thanks to the deafening football commentary on the TV and the fact that the flat was a loft arrangement, with the bedroom on a mezzanine floor.

We eventually had supper and I went to bed to more roars from the TV. This certainly was a day of two halves and I'd only experienced 'back of the net' once.

The next morning after breakfast we had the chance to talk properly – about hang-ups, life after divorce and coping with that and everything life throws at you. I couldn't understand how he could carry anger with him for so long, five years after his divorce and still fuming.

We spent the afternoon walking around Hampstead. I showed him my old school, I hadn't been there in years so it was poignant for me, boring for him. The afternoon was spent in front of the TV. Not a romantic film, but more Sky Sports. I fell asleep to the theme tune for 'Match of the Day' – *Der der der der da der da der da, der der de der de der...*

I left first thing Sunday morning, convinced that he wasn't really interested and I had badly misread the signals.

With hindsight I should have declined the invitation. I should have told him I was busy. But, in my defence, I really felt a connection with him and knew I needed to make a decision quickly, otherwise we would both have moved on.

If I'd waited it might have happened naturally. We should have enjoyed more shared experiences before sleeping together. But, in my opinion, sex is more important for men at the start of a relationship. Far more important than having adventures and experiences that don't involve getting naked.

After a few more meetings and over nights, we got to know each other a little better but with my continued juggling with work, Mum and Dad, finances, and him constantly travelling we started to drift apart.

After being in a relationship for over thirty years, it's inevitable that I have my own baggage. It's healthy to go through the long and often painful process of unburdening, while not coming across as a bitter and twisted wretch. But I don't need anyone else's.

I knew within minutes if a date was worth pursuing; not only as a relationship but also possible friendship, the important bit being able to spot the one's that wouldn't work. I could usually read what the guy thought as well. Like the date I met in a wine bar who, on seeing me, told the waitress to bring two (small) glasses and not a bottle. That's how keen he was for the date to be over. Barely able to make eye contact, he told me I was the same age as his wife (poor woman) and then asked me to 'drink up' quickly. Less than thirty minutes later we parted company at Green Park Tube Station. As I descended the steps down to the underground, I imagined the date sprinting up the road, putting as much distance between us as he could. I'm sure he'll find his 'younger model' eventually.

Thirty-Nine

It takes me all of one day to pack up my room at Spider House. Fiona is sulking with me and has been since I told her last week that I was moving out. No one month's notice here. Not if you're avoiding tax and generally an arse of the highest order.

As I was collecting my personal mug in the kitchen I spot Fiona's laptop open on the table; a dating site screen. My dating site. I know it's not *mine* but she only signed up because I had. Not one to be nosy I take a closer look and there, in among all the other hopeful middle-aged men, in all his fat bald headed glory, is William. She hasn't 'liked' him yet. I sense this is a work in progress. She is window shopping. I do her the favour of pressing 'Favourite'. Dare I send a message? I quickly type, "I love your sexy eyes. Do you like water sports? Let's meet. Soon as possible. XX." You're welcome, Fiona.

I can't get out of the house fast enough. I slam the front door, double lock and post the keys through the letter box.

Jenny is waiting for me in her car, packed with my belongings.

"Ready for a whole new chapter?" Yes, I nod. Definitely ready, because this chapter is going to be a good one.

My beautiful bed, towels, sheets, enough kitchen paraphernalia to feed six (forward planning) and the coffee table I love so much, my clothes, pictures, photographs and ornaments are all piled into the tiny flat. Jenny has given me a futon sofa and Lucy has unearthed a small dining table and two chairs. To me it was heaven on earth.

After Lucy, Jenny and Ed had left, I poured myself a glass of wine and, still in my slippers, take a short walk to Richmond Hill, with its amazing view over the river Thames. I sit on a bench and toast myself, my friends and the luck that had brought me to this point. Still another two years to pay off my debt, no man in my life but a great job and wonderful children. I savoured the moment.

I was joined five minutes into my 'moment savouring' by a homeless guy, clutching his own bottle of wine. We nod at one another and continue to admire the view.

"New to the area?" He's well spoken, and I wonder what has brought him to his personal situation. I also wonder if he thinks I'm homeless, what with the slippers and wine glass.

"Yes." I don't want to add anything. Here was a man who probably didn't need to hear about anyone else's problems.

"It's a good area. The bins are fruitful. So much waste. D'you know, I'd never eaten paté or quinoa until I became homeless in Richmond? Isn't that strange?" Good to know.

As I walk back to my flat I contemplate my future. I am now truly free. Free to come and go as I please without having to answer to anyone. I can jump on a bus to see mum or dad and know that, should there be an emergency, I am less than twenty minutes away. With only two years left to pay off my debt I am determined to get myself out there and have some fun.

Forty

I'm at my desk, working through one of my beloved spreadsheets when Sarah, my colleague, pokes her head around the door. "You busy?"

I pointedly look at the spreadsheet and surrounding chaos on my desk. She doesn't take the hint.

"Have you ever read a book called 'Yes Man' by Danny Wallace?"

"No, why? What is it? One of those Mills and Boon things?" Sarah loves a romance. All the heaving bosoms and tight breeches.

"No, it's about this guy who needs to get his life back on track, so he decides to say 'yes' to absolutely anything and everything. He does it for a whole month and nearly went mad, but it was a great experience. I think you should try it for a week and see what happens. Say Sunday to Sunday. Because I think you're being way too picky and not going out as much as you could. What do you think? Why aren't you joining in with this conversation?"

"Because, Sarah, you were stalked by a train driver who waved and toot-tooted you on the platform every morning for months and you ended up train hopping trying to shake him off. Taking relationship advice from you is difficult."

"Yes. okay. That was a bit scary."

Sarah chews the end of her pen for a few seconds.

"You don't have to say 'yes' to sex."

"Go away."

"The guy in the book turned his life around, you know."

I give up on the spreadsheet.

"I can't say 'yes' to every charity case I bump into in the street. I can't say 'yes' to every colleague looking for a sponsor on their parachute jump. I can't possibly say 'yes' to all sorts of things and expect to keep my job or not leave me penniless. Or put me in prison!"

"Well, how about you only apply it to, you know." Sarah points vaguely in the direction of my computer. "The online dating thing. The ones you 'Like' or whatever it is you do with them? Whatever they ask, that's not sex, you have to say 'yes.' yes?"

Christ, she's not going to drop this.

"Okay. I'll give it a go."

"You're lying. I can tell you're lying."

"Yes I am."

"Well, well. I never thought I'd see the day when Lizzie Watkins chickened out of a dare. Well, well, well, well... "

"I'LL DO IT! OKAY? NOW GO AWAY!"

Sarah smiles a smug smile. I scowl back at her.

I can't concentrate on my spreadsheet now. I've completely lost the thread. I open the online dating site. Just for a quick peak at the array of unappealing profile pictures. Not one of them a 'yes'. Sunday is going to be tricky.

Forty-One

"Is that Lizzie?" It was the care home.

"Yes, is Mum all right?"

"Yes, she's fine. We're actually calling about Paddy?"

Who the fuck is Paddy?

"There's been a bit of an incident."

I *knew* it. The orgies were true.

"She found Paddy in her room and assumed he was stealing."

"Oh, no!"

But isn't that what they do? Dementia sufferers steal stuff.

"She pushed him to the floor. We had to call an ambulance. He couldn't get up off the floor. His hip was broken."

Oh Mother.

"Oh, God. That's terrible. I don't know what to say. Should I send him some flowers? What ward is he in?" Honestly, my mother was prone to fight her own shadow when she was sane.

"He's died."

My mother is a murderer.

"Right. What happens now?"

"We've informed the police and the relatives, of course."

"Will she be arrested? Can a dementia sufferer go to prison?"

"You mustn't worry. They were with him when he died and they are not angry with Mum. She can't remember a thing about it. So, don't worry."

Yeah, right. I tried that once when I was stopped for speeding on the M3. Fail.

"Next time you visit we need to talk about your Mum's medication."

"Absolutely. Whatever you need to increase, or update or strengthen."

"No, it's not that. She's refusing to take it."

Of course. It wouldn't be anything else. It wouldn't be something easy, would it?

I call Nicky who wonders if she could give mum a 'whack list' of ex-boyfriends.

"It's not funny!"

"Oh, come on. It is a bit. This is a whole new level of bonkers!" Nicky says.

I'm thankful that I don't have to bail Mum out or visit the home. According to Patricia, Mum is currently dancing to 'Ernie, The Fastest Milkman in The West' by Benny Hill, so all was well on the care home front. I'm thankful because I have invited YM over to my little flat.

As soon as I'd moved in, he was the first person I'd wanted to show it off to. I'd made a light supper, bought some decent wine and even lit a few tea candles. He arrives and duly inspects every room, which took all of three minutes. He could see how excited I was and seemed genuinely pleased for me.

"I'm amazed you manage all this with so little money!" People with money always think like that, because they've had the good fortune (and no doubt sense) never to have been in that situation.

We had a lovely supper and ended up in bed. At least the sex was better now, despite my being told to shut up while 'doing it'. I seemed to laugh a lot which must be very off-putting for anyone.

Also, he didn't appreciate a running commentary. And that coming from a man whose entire free time was dominated by commentary, admittedly of the sporting variety, but, you know, let's not be picky.

On Sunday morning, we went for a long walk. I had a sense, despite our lovely evening, that we were just going to be friends and rather than continue wondering I decided to find out where I stood.

"Where do you think we're headed, relationship wise?" I asked.

I had low expectations and wasn't disappointed when he told me he saw the relationship as "very congenial". I knew, then and there that we had to stop seeing each other.

I waved him off a little while later and rushed back into the flat to google 'congenial', worried that my understanding of the word was wrong. Nope. Unfortunately, I was right.

I'm agreeable, pleasant. All the qualities for… I don't know, working in a library? Certainly not a 'come on baby light my fire' quality. I chalk that one up along with the other first of 'too posh'.

At least now with YM gone I can concentrate on this 'Say Yes' thing. Why have I agreed to do this? Because, weirdly, I need to. I want to put myself in situations and places I'd never been in before. I want to be challenged.

I arrive home and open the laptop.

"What delights do I have today?"

'HornyHenry7'

Plonker, with a disturbing set of photographs. I click 'favourite'. He messages almost immediately: "What side of the bed do you sleep on?"

Oh please. That's not something I need to respond to with a 'Yes'? I send "Piss off, yes?" That should be clear enough.

'Scotsman72'.

'Favourite'.

Message: "So Hen, are you posh? I went to Fettes. Do you know it? A very posh school in Scotland."

Ooh, maybe I can be my 'posh' self then.

"Tony Blair went to the same school. Which school did you go to?"

I reply "I'm not posh. I have a tattoo of Tony Blair on my back."

I wasn't travelling to bloody Scotland on the basis of a 'yes.'

'OutofSynch69'

Hmm. No photographs. But he's liked me. I 'favourite' back.

He messages me (I'm getting the distinct impression that every single man over the age of fifty five is sitting at his computer browsing websites right now.)

"Well hello there. I wondered how long it would take for you to give in".

To what? Death?

"So, sweet lady. My first question is 'bath or shower?"

"Shower." Damn. That's very Psycho. I should have said bath.

"I'm looking for someone to share a bath with at the end of every day. It's the only way I can really communicate with a woman so fairly crucial I get this right from the start"

Thank Christ I didn't say bath.

"Good luck with that. Maybe change user name to 'OutofSink69'?"

'naturelover55'

Kind, smiley face. I 'favourite' him.

He messages:

"Is it me or is everyone over the age of fifty five browsing dating sites today?"

"I think it's replaced going to church." I reply, hoping he's not a lonely vicar.

I wait, tapping impatiently on the keyboard.

"Would you like to meet for a coffee or a tea one day?"

"Yes, I would. On condition, we have cake as well."

"I think I can manage that. Just the one slice, mind."

We swap email addresses, his name is Andy, and exchange a few messages. We arrange to meet for coffee on Tuesday.

I shut down my laptop and settle down for an evening of wine and a good film. I'm happy that I've ended on a 'high'; a 'low' being someone with no teeth and a passion for carp fishing. I'm quite looking forward to meeting 'naturelover'.

Forty-Two

As I get ready for work the next morning I get an email from 'naturelover'.

> *I'm sorry to be a pain but I won't be able to make our coffee on Tuesday.*

Knew it. Probably got a better offer. I read on.

> *I don't suppose you would like to be my date for a dinner I have been invited to? It's a very relaxed do. No need to dress up.*

Dinner means no quick escape. Dinner means enduring other people. Dinner means hard work. I need more details. I have to say 'Yes',

> *Love to. Send me the details later. I need to catch my train.*

I sign off with my name and mobile number.

I've stepped off the cliff and, so far, haven't hit anything on the way down or even landed. Maybe I'm flying. Maybe I need help.

He doesn't call all day. Maybe he's changed his mind. Or maybe he's decided to wait until I'm fifteen minutes into my 'leave for twenty minutes' home hair dye kit. Yep.

"Hi. How lovely to talk to you and thank you so much for agreeing to be my date. It's on Saturday and it's a…"

I cut in "Can I call you back? Just… cooking… something…"

"Yes. Of course." I hear the doubt in his voice. He thinks I'm mad.

I hang up. Wait for the remaining minutes to pass before washing the dye out of my hair and admiring the orange hue. Some would call that strawberry blonde. Others would call it a cock up. I don't care.

I call him back "Sorry. I had to baste something."

"That's fine" he says "We all need to baste something once in a while."

I find this hysterical and laugh like a drain. I know I'm not making the right impression. Top marks to him though as he ploughs on.

"So, this thing on Saturday, it's a birthday party for a good friend of mine. It's at a lovely seaside hotel, we have the run of the entire place. There will be about forty guests in total. Most of us are naturists…"

He's talking but I can't hear the words. It's just a white noise as I stare into the middle distance. Did he say 'hotel'? Did he say 'naturist'? I tune back in.

"Hello? You still there? Did you faint?" He laughs. I laugh. Oh how we laugh. He gets that a lot, apparently, people shocked into silence. But I was shocked into deafness. That is new, he says.

"Please don't think that you have to strip off."

I realise the hair on my head doesn't match my pubes. Or, as Mum used to say, 'That woman's collar and cuffs don't match,' when she spotted a bad hair-dye job.

"As it's clearly your first time…'

You think?

"You can keep your underwear on. That is perfectly acceptable…"

There's a lengthy silence, occasionally filled with my heavy nasal breathing. God knows what he thought *that* was down to. Eventually I found my voice.

"Well, you're right about one thing. It certainly is my first time. And yes, I *will* be keeping my underwear on."

He was delighted. "You'll come?" An innocent enough question, I hoped, not one loaded with innuendo.

I hang up and pace. I pace while drying my orange hair. I pace while having a shower. I pace while washing up. All the while convincing myself I can do this. It's only underwear. Just like wearing a bikini… surrounded by naked people. Normal. Nothing to see here, plenty to see over there. I'll pretend it's a Lucy event and I'm just socialising.

Where are we? Monday. I have until Saturday to sort myself out. Four days to get a grip and psych myself up. First I need to know what the latest trend is for lady garden topiary/minge fashion – who can I ask? Lucy, obviously. I race round to her flat and thankfully find her in, lounging on the sofa, flicking through a magazine. "Hi Ma. What's up?"

"Don't move. I need to show you something." I dive into her bedroom, strip off and return, wearing her dressing gown. Flinging open the gown I ask, as calmly as I can

"Does this need sorting?"

Quick lifting of eyes from her magazine she peruses my bush like she's checking out the price of eggs. She indicates, using her hands, that I should "narrow the field".

"Thanks, gorgeous."

Back into the bedroom, into clothes and out of the door, having been waved off with the words

"Whoever the lucky man is, I hope he appreciates your efforts."

The next day I make an array of appointments, practically sobbing at the cost of a visit to the hairdressers, waxing lady and tanning salon. I'm going to kill Sarah.

During my lunch-hour I go in search of some reasonably priced underwear. I didn't want to look like Miss Whiplash but equally I did not want to be mistaken for Miss Marple.

I ended up picking matching black bra and pants from M and S. An outfit any woman would be proud of, be it in A and E or a naturist party. It said 'respect' mixed with 'maybe not'. I still felt incredibly vulnerable when I checked myself out that evening.

I'll take the biggest handbag I own. Held in the right way it covers me from shoulder to waist and get me to the dining table without revealing too much. I practise. Wearing my underwear, I sashay from my tiny kitchen into the living room, realising too late, that I haven't drawn the curtains and given the couple living opposite something to talk about over their Merlot.

I imagine that, once seated with a napkin (hopefully a large linen one) draped over my lap, things won't be so bad. I pray the hotel's well heated. I could always ask for more napkins. If I get enough napkins I could make a toga.

During the tanning and waxing I send Sarah endless text messages outlining the different ways I'm going to torture her, how much I hate her and that our friendship is over. "Pictures! I want pictures!" was her constant reply.

The day arrives. Twenty four hours from now this will be over. Not only the sodding party but also the 'Say Yes' challenge.

I can't quite believe I'm going through with this. "I can always back out and pretend I'd gone through with it" kept going round and round in my head. I could lie to Sarah and just send her a picture of me in my pants, glass of G and T in my hand, in a dimly lit room.

Andy met me at the station. I don't know why I was surprised he was fully clothed but he was and I was hugely relieved. We went for a drink in a nearby pub, not only to calm my nerves but also to get to know each other a little. He was attentive and very funny, with tales of disastrous naturist moments: ants nest, unattended candles and hair spray to name but a few. He was a lovely guy and I immediately felt that this naturist thing was far more to do with feeling liberated and not at all sleazy. Lucy would certainly get on with this guy.

When we finally arrive at the hotel I am directed to the ladies changing room where, I am told, I will find Rachel, wife of the birthday boy.

I open the door, turn the corner and am faced with a row of naked bottoms, all lined up at the basins. I yelp in surprise and embarrassment. My instinct was to apologise and rush out except they all turn to see where the yelp came from and now I am faced with, what seemed like, dozens of boobs.

'You must be Lizzie!' said one, phenomenally well endowed, lady.

'Rachel?' I asked, eyes firmly fixed on her hairline. She laughs and gives me a reassuring pat on the arm.

The other ladies turned back to the mirrors and continue with their make-up and hair.

'I know. It's a shocker at first. You just don't know where to look!' Rachel was kind and funny. She shows me to the lockers, where I can put my clothes.

"I'll get you a G and T. Double?"

"Yes! Please." I'm left alone to get ready in my own time. This really is bizarre. I feel out of place for being dressed.

I shut myself in the loo and undress. I can hear the normal sort of female chatter about children, jobs, men, illnesses et cetera. Maybe I could just stay in the loo. Rachel hands me the G&T under the toilet door. I down it in one. Then, taking a breath, I open the door. Da daaaaah! No one batted an eyelid. In fact, none of them even glanced at me. The least they could do was compliment me on my lacy knickers!

The ladies and I leave the loos as one. Rachel beside me, her boobs wobbling alarmingly. We meet the gentlemen in the dining room. I managed to stifle my yelp this time, mainly because I desperately wanted to laugh out loud. Pot-bellied, skinny, short, tall, big willies, small willies, acorns, man boobs, hairy bits, bald bits – all magnificently and unashamedly on display. I tell you it brought a tear to my eye.

Andy meets me at the door and introduces me to the birthday boy. Am I the only one who finds it so hard to look people in the face? My eyes keep being drawn to bits, balls and boobs. My fascination is purely scientific, of course.

I am suddenly very hungry and am relieved when dinner is called. I follow Andy into the dining room, clutching my large handbag. It's a buffet that, I was horrified to notice, was level with most of the men's willies and I couldn't help but notice more than one testicle dragging along the edge of the tablecloth. I resisted the urge to shout "Unexpected item in the bagging area" and avoided all the dishes at the front of the table, taking only from the dishes I could reach.

Everyone is so incredibly friendly and, after spotting a couple of other ladies in underwear, I started to relax.

The people on my table are great fun and, apart from one lady accidentally dipping her nipple in the sauce as she stretched across the table, no one spoke about nudity.

Thinking about it, the lead up to the event was the scariest thing about it. The event itself was fun, enlightening and memorable to say the least. Other than uncomfortable wooden seats and the thought that people were placing bare bottoms on God Knows What in the germ department, I thoroughly enjoyed myself.

When Andy and I finally parted company, both fully clothed, I knew that we would not be meeting again. My world would always be fully clothed and no argument would change that. I had learned something about myself though. I would do anything to make my family and friends laugh their heads off and know that I would always be all right.

Forty-Three

Mum was going rapidly downhill. She was refusing to take her medication which meant either Nicky or I had to visit the home early in the morning, every day for a week, to force her to take her medication. And 'force' is the right word. We tried to hide tablets in a biscuit (custard creams were the biscuits of choice – easy to pry apart and bury the tablet in the cream) or crumble the tablets up in her tea. The crumbling in tea was quickly knocked on the head by Patricia. The tablets were 'slow release'. I'll tell you what was 'slow release' – getting out of the sodding home before eight o'clock.

It was exhausting, trying not to make Mum feel rushed but knowing I had to get to work. We knew Mum would assume we were going to stay for a few hours so the dreaded moment of departure was doubly difficult with the inevitable outburst or tears, anger and insults. I felt guilty because I was leaving to go to work, guilty because I arrived late for work and then guilty that I was leaving work early to go and check on Dad/shop/visit Mum. It felt as if this would never end.

One week turned into two and then three. The early morning tablet coaxing went on for over a month. Mum, institutionalised by now, was giving up.

She had always had a fear of water so it was left to me and Nicky to bathe Mum. She became hysterical if any of the staff at the care home tried. Treating her like a frightened child, we chatted to her while running a shallow bath and undressing her. Nicky and I managed to keep it together long enough, lowering this tiny, trembling old lady onto the bath seat and gently washing her, telling her that very soon she would be in her pyjamas with a lovely cup of tea and a biscuit. Washing her hair was difficult as panic set in when the water ran down her face. She'd fight us, cry, shout for help, but then it was over. We dried and dressed her. Brushed her hair. After yet another traumatic farewell Nicky and I went straight to the nearest pub.

Mum spent a lot of time sleeping. Dad would still visit and sit by her bed but his visits were no longer daily outings. He also wanted to sleep, sitting in front of his television.

I received a call one Sunday from Patricia. Mum has been taken to Kingston Hospital. A niggly chest infection wasn't responding to medication. In other words, Mum wasn't taking the medication for the chest infection.

I drove to the hospital and was told by a very young doctor that Mum was very sick. I called Nicky and the children to let them know what was happening. Looking at this tiny old lady, lying on a hospital bed, semi-conscious with such a frightened expression on her pale face, I knew we were looking at the end of the road for Mum.

She was diagnosed with pneumonia and placed on an open ward.

I sat with her, holding her hand, listening to her laboured breathing. It would have been peaceful if it weren't for the guy in the opposite bed shouting

"My colon! My colon!"

I asked the nurse what was wrong with him and she replied, with a wry smile "Constipated and a man. Need I say more?"

Mum, who was still aware of everything going on around her, mustered all her energy to say "If you don't shut up about your bloody colon, I'll come over and sort you out myself." Amazingly, he stopped shouting.

I left Mum, secure in the knowledge that she was too unwell to get out of bed, let alone wander around the wards. How wrong was I? According to the nurse who answered the phone when I rang to check on Mum she was up and down like a yoyo as soon as I'd left. After hearing that I couldn't settle either, drove back to the hospital at ten o'clock that night.

I sneaked past the quiet sleepy wards to Mum's bed. The curtains were drawn. For an awful stomach churning moment, I thought she'd died. I peeped around the curtains and saw a nurse holding Mum's hand, stroking her hair and singing to her like a child. I said nothing. Just smiled at the nurse, walked out of the hospital, got into my car and sobbed. Say what you will about the NHS, the patience and care given by that nurse was brilliant and I will always be grateful to her.

The next morning Mum was moved into a palliative care ward. Her health had deteriorated significantly overnight. I was familiar with palliative care, having witnessed it at St James', and I was hoping it would be more, or less, the same kind of treatment. Calm, peaceful and friendly.

With Mum semi-conscious in her hospital bed, the porter came to take Mum up to the palliative care ward, telling us we couldn't travel with her in the lift and that we should find our own way to the ward. Nicky, Jenny – who'd raced over to be with us, charged up the stairs, eager to be at the lift when Mum arrived. I announced Mum's imminent arrival to the staff, but no one knew who we were or who Mum was. Not a brilliant start.

The lift doors opened and Mum appeared with the porter and, after waiting a few minutes, with all of us lurking in the corridor, watching staff come and go, I suggested that at the very least she be placed in one of the rooms for a bit of privacy.

A nurse came in and took her pulse and then left. We waited, admiring the strangers name above Mum's bed. Who knows where that person had gone. Probably to the 'other side'. By now Mum was awake, confused, crying and in pain. I went out into the corridor and shouted,

"Anyone interested in my Mother?"

A young female doctor came in and said

"Sorry, who are you? We can't give out medication if the patient isn't our patient".

"WELL GO AND FIND OUT WHO IS BLOODY WELL LOOKING AFTER MY MOTHER AND GIVE HER PAIN RELIEF," was my measured response.

I was horrified with my reaction. Jenny was upset, but we all wanted the same thing. A peaceful end for Mum. We were told Mum's nurse was on her break.

"What do you mean her nurse is on her break? For God's sake get someone in here who knows what they are doing."

Eventually Mum was given morphine and she calmed down. With Nicky on one side of the bed and me on the other, I talked to Mum about moving into a house where there were no men to annoy us. That was always something Mum talked about when she was angry with Dad. I told her I'd do the cooking while Nicky washed up. Mum would be in charge of the garden. I have no idea whether she could hear me but it was a very calm moment for all of us.

Just as the evening sun was setting and the birds had stopped tweeting, Mum slipped away. That sounds so corny but it was true. The sense of relief and, bizarrely, euphoria was immense. Knowing that Mum was no longer in pain, no longer living in a waking nightmare, was a great comfort. If our 'young Mum' had known that the end of her life would turn out this way she probably would have opted to kill herself.

If we were upset about anything, it was the battle with staff to make the end as painless as possible for Mum. Jenny was extremely upset. Not only because her grandmother had died but the *way* in which she died. Watching her mother yelling at people in the corridor, trying to get pain relief, Nicky yelling at two doctors so busy flirting with each other that they forgot what their jobs were.

Finally, a sense of calm descended on the room and, when a male nurse came in to take Mum's blood pressure we all silently watched. Glancing at each other with disbelief and just about managing to hold back tears of laughter.

The nurse took Mum's blood pressure and looked at us in shock when he couldn't get a reading. I think the expressions on our faces told him that we already knew. He shuffled out of the room with a mumbled apology.

Nicky fetched Dad from his flat and took him to see Mum. He mewed like a lost puppy, patting Mum's hand, kissing her, stroking her hair. Eventually we took him away. We had lunch in a nearby pub and, as we drove Dad back to his flat, one of the strangest things happened. Mum's favourite song came on the radio. "Strangers on the shore" by Acker Bilk.

A lot of people came to Mum's funeral. People we hadn't seen for a very long time which was wonderful. Mum had always assumed that people flocked to see Dad so she would have been so surprised and overwhelmed that they were there for her.

We collected Dad in a funeral car for the service but I wasn't sure he knew what we were all doing and who we were mourning. Even with the Order of Service in his hand and turning it over so that he could see the lovely picture of Mum on the back, I'm still not sure he fully understood. Sitting in the front row of the mortuary, he looked around, occasionally pointing and giving the thumbs up sign to someone he recognised. Some of these people were in tears for Dad too, seeing Dad after such a long time and noticing how frail he was.

Dad was tired and confused by the end of the service and it was beginning to get cold so we took him home straight after that. We got him ready for bed and sat him in front of a John Wayne film with a cup of tea and sandwiches, promising to come back later.

The staff at the care home had been so fond of Mum that they laid on a wonderful wake. We headed back there and shared some lovely memories with Mum's family and friends.

I picked up Mum's ashes a week later and decided to keep them on the mantelpiece in my flat with some fairy lights draped around them, until we all decided what to do with them.

One evening Nicky came round to discuss where we should scatter Mum – the Thames? Mum was an East End girl, she might like that. Richmond Park? Mum liked going for walks there? The sea? Suddenly the fairy lights fell off the mantel piece. Nicky and I literally leapt a foot in the air. Not the sea then.

Some weeks later, on a beautifully sunny day, we gathered to scatter Mum's ashes in Richmond Park, the place where we used to meet up for family picnics. It was one of those weird moments when no one quite knew what to do. I had the urn so I tipped a bit of Mum into everyone's hands. I don't know why I did that. Maybe I thought everyone would like to say their own personal goodbye. We'd all had such different relationships with Mum and maybe needed to whisper our own goodbye. I did re-think that as we walked to the café for tea with bits of Mum still on our hands and shoes but it was too late.

It was a sad but positive day.

Forty-Four

Yorkshireman and I still saw each other, on and off, but it was nothing serious. In a way, it was the best relationship I never had. A male friend willing to listen to me ranting about some date or other. He could do the same; whenever any of his dates went pear-shaped he could email or phone me. I knew his heart wasn't really in it – he had no intention of finding 'the one'. He liked the chase but would get tangled up in the specifics: their home – how would it work if they moved in together? their money – it's such a mess and I'm so organised – their children – I really don't want the responsibility. Honestly, I don't think he knew what he wanted at all.

The best thing about this 'non-relationship' was the friendship we'd formed. We really were besties, which is why I asked him to be my date at a black-tie dinner at the Natural History Museum. This was a huge step for me. I'd only ever been to black-tie functions with William. This was my first time going rogue, so I was excited when he turned up looking his usual sleepy, pre-occupied self which I bizarrely found very sexy.

The event was sponsored by Courvoisier, renowned for their 'blow your head off' cognac, and Lucy had put a table of twelve together. The evening was going well until Lucy opened the giant bottle of Courvoisier that was, in fact, the table centre piece. I was on my third glass of cognac, having already had endless glasses of wine, when the auction started.

To this day I have no idea why I ended up bidding for a Banksy painting. Okay, that's a lie. I was raging with alcohol and on an emotional high, that's why my hand shot up. To make matters worse I was bidding against someone else on our table. If they'd been at a table on the other side of the room I'm pretty sure Lucy would have broken my arm – anything to stop me bid and bid and bid. The more people laughed and gasped, the more I bid, £7,000, £8,000, £9,000. Then, to my horror…

"To the lady on my left, £10,000 Banksy. Thank you so much!"

Before I could take a breath, a charity lady swooped down on me with her clipboard to take my details. Full of the joys of cognac and buoyed by a sense of insanity, I glanced over to Yorkshireman. He was staring at me in absolute horror.

Lucy took the clipboard from me and handed it to a footballer sitting at our table.

"Here, you could do with some decent artwork on your wall." Bless his knee-high cotton socks, he happily gave over his details to the perplexed charity lady.

But for me, the damage was done. Yorkshireman was sitting next to a hard-drinking loose cannon and he wanted to distance himself as soon as possible.

I remember being helped out of the venue, down the steps and into a waiting cab. With money handed over to the driver with strict instructions to get me home and wait until I'm through my front door, I saw YM leap into the cab behind me. He must have told the driver not to spare the horses because he was gone before I'd had a chance to breathe a cognac fuelled farewell in his face. As the cab drove away I shouted for him to stop

"I SHOULD BE IN HIS CAB NOT THIS ONE" I yelled but it was not to be. I knew I'd blown any chance I had of keeping this friendship.

YM texted me the next day. "We need to talk." He wasn't cross that I had bid. He was cross that he had been put in a position of possibly having to part with ten thousand pounds and he didn't particularly want a Banksy painting. I knew I should have bid for the 'Weekend for Two' but even then he'd only have gone with me if Sky Sports was available.

Forty-Five

None of us could escape the fact that Dad was now as fragile as Mum was a year ago. What made it so much more difficult was the inability to communicate with him. Scribbled notes, if he could be bothered to scribble at all, didn't make sense now. He could no longer feed himself and was consequently losing weight at an alarming rate. His ability to care for himself was almost non-existent.

His inhibitions had also vanished. He would expose himself at the drop of a hat (or trouser). If only he had a hat to cover himself it wouldn't have been quite so bad. He liked being naked a lot of the time and unless arm wrestled into clothes would have wandered off in that state. The manager of the retirement home was constantly calling to pass on some drama or other, usually involving dad flooding his bathroom or the smell coming from Dad's flat. The woman living opposite Dad would hammer on his door, demanding he turn his TV down and/or turn the bath tap off (he had a habit of leaving it running all night).

Dad also took to wandering around town, and things came to a head when, one evening the manager of a pub nearby said he saw dad walk past the pub wall and thought, "What a smart gent, with his shirt, tie and regimental blazer." That was until the pub wall ended and he could see the bottom half. Naked. Absolutely nothing on between the blazer and his highly polished shoes and socks. The police were called and, once again, Dad was picked up and taken home. Praise where praise is due. His top half was immaculate.

Going from an amusing raconteur, full of life, constantly phoning and emailing friends and family, Dad slipped into a deep depression, not wanting to go anywhere or be seen by anyone. The thought of being just a bystander at events was not his way.

Within three months of Mum's funeral, I could see Dad was giving up on life. Watching him disintegrate so rapidly was painful and I was back to feeling guilty that I wasn't there to help him every day. I also felt uncontrollable anger that this was happening to us again and it all just seemed to be never ending. Dad wouldn't want to have lived like this. He made me promise not to put him in a home. When he could still doodle notes he had written, "I no home", and I had just given him the thumbs up, knowing it was inevitable.

We organised home care, to check on him each morning and evening, preparing a meal, hoping this would also make our lives easier, but could never be sure just how long the carer stayed with him or whether he had finished the meal prepared. He would often shoo them out of the door and notes in their log book would confirm that he was completely ignoring them and the food most of the time.

I remember a moment when Nicky and I called in one evening and Dad was asleep in his chair. Nicky whispered,

"Please God let him be dead. That would be a good way to go, wouldn't it?"

"No!" I hissed back. "Everyone would think we killed him."

"Maybe if we just pinched his nose?" Nicky suggested.

"Have you seen the size of Dad's nose? That's a two-man job."

We looked at him, fast asleep in his chair, remote control clasped in his hand.

"I'll put the kettle on then." Nicky whispered, as I set about microwaving some faggots for Dad.

Forty-Six

What is it about Lucy that makes me cave in at the first hurdle?

"What could go wrong Ma. Just meet up and see if you get along."

It's a blind date with someone who had quite clearly hit on her – 'her' being a six-foot blonde and thirty years younger than me.

Dave had been sitting outside a pub one evening on the Fulham Road when he saw Lucy cycle past. She was meeting friends at a café nearby and chained up her bike outside. When she returned she had found a post-it note on her handlebars. It said,

"I've never done this before but think you look so lovely and wonder whether you would like to meet up. My number is… I hope you are up for a meeting."

She thought it was rather sweet and old fashioned so she called him the next day. After a flirty conversation, she asked how old he was and, when told he was in his fifties she suggested he might like to meet me, her *mother.* I am nearer his age and single. Well, presumably to get to the daughter you need to get past the mother first so he agreed. A day and time was set and then I was told. Very thoughtful of her.

I was having fun with an ex-police Inspector at the time. Not *that* kind of fun but just meeting up and laughing more than I'd ever laughed. He had the best stories; thirty years in the police force, he'd seen everything but he suddenly found himself retired and alone, which wasn't so funny. We didn't dwell on that too much. However, despite being cross with Lucy for taking it upon herself to sort out my love life, I agreed to meet 'Post-it note man' in the Fulham Road pub where he'd first seen Lucy.

Hopping onto a bus after work one evening I arrived at the pub and walked in, on the dot of the agreed time of seven thirty. He was standing in the middle of the pub, clutching a single rose and watching the door. It felt like a play; I was the leading female but hadn't been given the script.

The punters, on either side of the room, were the audience, watching the man with the rose. Maybe there's a trapdoor that I can disappear into. I advanced, smiling and making eye contact. I kissed him on the cheek and took hold of his hand.

"There's a cracking pub on the other side of the green. Let's go there".

Within the space of roughly twenty seconds I had managed to introduce myself, grab rose, grab man and get him out of the door. Who knows what happened back in the bar area. Did they applaud or did I just imagine that? Who cares. All that mattered was that we'd escaped that pub.

I should have given him that one evening and left it at that. He told me he was still married, very recently split from his cheating wife and this was his first date with another woman. To be honest, I didn't fancy him, he was funny and attentive; maybe that's why I agreed to see him again. I also felt sorry for him and had a weird sense of obligation to see him through the difficult first steps of 'getting out there.'

After a few more casual meetings I realised he was only pretending to move on. He clearly didn't want to leave the 'happy' home. I heard from a mutual friend that he hadn't moved out of the marital home and that he was leaving post-it notes around the house declaring his love for his wife. I was beginning to feel like a counsellor every time we met.

He'd always 'just eaten'. So, not wishing to be rude by eating alone in front of him, I found myself starving until I got home and devoured a bowl of Corn Flakes. Often, I was too tired to eat anything at all once I got home. He didn't pay for anything either. I told Nicky about this. She told me to leave my wallet at home. See how he liked that. The thought of going out without my purse was too painful, so I tucked a twenty pound note into my back pocket. Just in case.

We were sitting in a lovely hotel bar on Chelsea Harbour, when I told him that I had left my purse at home, he suggested that "just for fun" we bolted out of the door without paying.

I couldn't do that. I work near this place and have been here with clients. I 'magically' found the twenty pound note which just covered the cost of our coffees (no tip). I reported back to Nicky. She suggested that I "dumped the stingy twat!"

He was still obsessed with Lucy. I didn't mind. Never one to be jealous anyway, and certainly not of my children, I took him along to a charity event organised by Lucy. It was full on fancy dress. He wanted to be young again. He wanted to flirt and do all the things he hadn't been able to do as 'husband of'. He dressed as Mickey Mouse and once he'd spotted a 'Minnie', he was off. I was happy to sit and chat to Lucy's friends until he came back. Mickey had lost his tail.

Another Lucy charity event saw him dressed head to toe in one of those ghastly lyrcra morph outfits. Fine, if you're a rugby type with muscles, but he resembled a pop sock full of walnuts. Worse still, when he very obviously became excited, his little todger stood to attention, looking like a pencil with a rubber on the end. This man was good fun but not for me. I decided it was time for him to go his own way.

We met again a week later and over coffees I knew I'd be paying for, I told him I didn't want to see him again.

"But what shall I do now?"

"Go back to your wife?" seemed like the obvious solution to me. "You've never actually left her, have you? You're both playing games. Time to get over yourselves."

I'd had enough of listening to him trying to be clever and funny. I was bored with the feeble excuses of why he couldn't pay for a coffee. I was sick of spending my hard-earned money on someone who really should have been able to pay his way. I found his relationship with his wife, with them both 'playing away' really depressing. In my old-fashioned opinion, an affair isn't something to be gotten over. It's something that should be prevented and that takes hard work and commitment from both sides.

Forty-Seven

Nicky and I were on the third care home. The previous two had already pushed us into a deep well of depression; they had been smelly, characterless, dirty, and shabby. The 'no' boxes were outweighing the 'yes' ones by a long chalk. Dad needed full time care. Still determined to remain independent, he was a hot-ring away from a full-on house fire, thanks to his continuing attempts at cooking his own meals.

Deciding we could save the visit to care home number four for another day we stopped off at the pub around the corner from Dad's flat. We needed a moment to regroup and breathing in wine fumes help alleviate the stench of urine that seemed to cling to our clothes before going around to Dad and cooking his evening meal.

Nicky had her laptop with her and was looking for more homes to visit. She found some new ones, made notes of contact numbers and email addresses.

"Dad's going to hate us."

"I know, but we don't have any choice, do we? He's a danger to himself."

"Can't we just drive him out to the countryside and let him roam free?" asked Nicky.

"Remind me never to buy you a puppy for Christmas," I said.

The smell emanating from Dad's flat, as we make our way along the corridor to his front door, is shocking. I can't help but be embarrassed for him.

We let ourselves in. The flat is completely quiet and our first thought, once we'd got over the soaking wet carpets – Dad has left the shower running again – was that Dad had gone walkabout.

"Well at least he hasn't set fire to the place." Nicky says, while stepping over a puddle.

We peer into the living room and see Dad, sitting in his favourite chair, pad and pencil in hand. The TV is on mute. Eggheads.

"All right Dad?" I yell.

We think he's concentrating on whatever it is he's trying to write but, as we approach we realise his eyes are closed. He's not breathing. Cold to the touch.

I kneel beside his chair and gently take the pad and pencil. With his shaky hand writing he's written

"My wife. I love."

As heartbroken as we were, the next two weeks were spent on organising the funeral and contacting all Dad's friends and family and trying to erase all smells in the flat before putting it on the market. We spent hours going through old photographs and letters and a lot of time was spent making cups of tea to stop the tears. Of course the cat had to go. As Nicky had bought it in the first place, she took on the responsibility of taking it to a cats' home.

When she came back with the empty basket, I didn't ask what had happened and she didn't offer any explanation either. It just added to the sadness.

The Guards Chapel was filled with Mum and Dad's friends and extended family. Dad would have been so proud and thankful that we managed to give him such a good send off. So many people of all ranks were there, the Regimental Band played his favourite tunes, the order of service was moving and, now and then, quite funny.

Just close family went to the crematorium at Mortlake. It was better that way and meant we could either go straight home or head for the pub to join everyone else, depending on how we felt.

I couldn't believe this indestructible, charismatic, funny and infuriating man, my Dad, was gone.

I returned to my flat, completely exhausted and broken. It was as if I'd run out of petrol. I was in limbo.

I spoke briefly to my boss who told me to take as long as I needed and so, after pouring myself a glass of wine, I dragged my duvet to the sofa and crawled underneath it. I stayed there for three whole days, only getting up for a pee or to make a cup of tea. I watched crap TV and got a worrying crush on Jeremy Kyle…that's how bad it was. Guessing whether the aunt/mother/sister/girlfriend was indeed having it away with the son/boyfriend/father/uncle was the highlight of my day. Waiting for the lie detector results almost tipped me over the edge.

On day three I received a text from Yorkshireman asking how I was. I just sent a text back saying

'Have lost my lovely Dad.'

He phoned me straight away.

"I'm picking you up tomorrow morning. We'll go for a walk." I didn't want him to. He was a banker. They don't take time off during the week. Certainly not this one. The world would stop turning and I couldn't cope with the guilt of the world not turning.

I just wanted to wallow for a bit longer but he wouldn't take *No* for an answer. I hauled myself up off the sofa, showered, ate the things in the fridge that hadn't grown mould and went to bed for a good night's sleep.

I half expected YM not to turn up. I thought something financial and important would get in the way at the last minute and, honestly, I wouldn't have minded. But he did turn up. And we did go for a very long walk.

I have no idea what we talked about as we walked along the riverside. I do remember going from laughing to crying to talking and back again for hours on end. There was something different between us. We were listening to each other, really listening. I felt completely at ease, pouring out all the things that had happened over the last couple of months with Dad, work and anything else that tumbled out of me.

We went back to my flat and YM stayed the night. Nothing happened. He just held me. It was the best sleep I'd had for a very long time.

Before he left for work, early the next morning, YM told me that he'd be visiting Cairo in January for a conference – something clever and vital to do with investments – and straight over my head.

"Would you like to join me after the conference? Show me the real Cairo? I'll cover everything, the fares and such like."

I'd lived in Cairo for four years. I knew it like the back of my hand. I knew we were just friends but the thought of spending time with someone I trusted completely, in such a lovely part of the world was the most exciting thing EVER. I just had to make it through Christmas and New Year.

Forty-Eight

Ed was determined that I didn't spend Christmas on my own so he booked us into the local pub for an 'all bells and whistles' Christmas lunch. After that we vegged out in front of the TV and watched awful films. I released him late in the afternoon; he'd done his duty and wonderfully so but the poor guy needed to be with his friends and get pissed.

YM called and wished me a happy Christmas too and we talked about Cairo, where we'd go, what we'd do. I was crossing the days off my calendar. Twenty days to go.

The period between Christmas and New Year is always a faffy, pointless bit of time. No one really does any work, except retailers and they all deserve medals for coping with the Sales that kick off on Boxing Day. There's panic buying of party dresses and a desperate hope that the invitation you've accepted is for a good knees-up and not some boring duff event. Then, there are the hollow expectations, the false hope, forced jollity and *kissing*.

This year it was particularly difficult. Nicky and I felt bereft, aimless. We harped on, to anyone willing to listen, that we were 'orphans' and, any time either one of us messed up – spilt something, dropped something, forgot something – we blamed it on 'grieving'. We laughed a lot, often to the point of hysteria. I suppose we were a bit delirious with relief – not having to worry about Mum or Dad.

To avoid the New Year nonsense Nicky and I decided to treat ourselves to a good old fashioned 'day out'. A drive out of London, a long walk, pub lunch and then a long meandering drive back to my flat. By then we'd be too knackered to care about seeing in the New Year.

We put our wellies and a packed lunch in the boot of the Battered Bitch, on the off chance pubs might be too full or closed. We were so desperate to get out of London we would have happily sat in a field and had a picnic, rain or shine.

"Ready?" I ask Nicky.

"Yes!" she says, stabbing a destination I'd never heard of into the satnav.

"This is all a bit Thelma and Louise. You're not going to drive us off a cliff, are you? Coz I have a load of laundry to do."

I turn the key in the ignition. The Battered Bitch lets out one of her familiar shrieks, then shudders before… nothing. I try again and get a dry cough.

"Have you put petrol in?"

I squint at Nicky. "Shut up."

"F-U-U-U-U-C-K."

I try the key one more time and get nothing. Absolutely nothing.

"Richmond Hill?" I look at Nicky. So, with wellies on and picnic tucked into Nicky's rucksack, I don't even bother locking the car as we head off up the hill.

After an extremely long walk down to and along the River, we headed back up to pick our bench for the evening. We had a great time as it turned out; not only did my homeless person turn up with his recent bin pickings, but we ended up 'joining blankets' with other people, young and old, escaping the New Year's madness. With the river spread out before us we could see all the fireworks set off from houses and parks. Better than any paid event, for sure.

Forty-Nine

Eleven more days to go until I fly away. Cue me singing 'I Believe I Can Fly' around the flat until the miserable cow downstairs bangs on the ceiling with her broom stick. Witchy bitch. Although I'm not as bad as the woman in the downstairs flat at the back, who practises her piano almost every day. She's a professional pianist, so the playing is outstanding, I don't have a problem with that; in fact, I love it.

Whenever Nicky comes over we sit at the enormous living room window and smoke a fag, drink tea, and moan about everything and everyone. Luckily neither of us has inherited Dad's nose but we have inherited his sharp sense of humour and constant mickey taking of others, especially those who take themselves too seriously. We could both win Mum's gold medal for sulking and are quick to judge others. We can bitch about each other but anyone else tries it and they are shot down in flames; we get it from Mum. Family come first. It's not always a good thing but that's how we were and I had passed that on to my children.

Another favourite pastime we had was spying. okay, not exactly spying, more being nosey. Sitting in the window we could see straight in to the properties opposite. Opposite and to the right, in one of the flats, lived an older couple who held hands on the sofa, watching television from seven o'clock until nine thirty when they then went to bed. Opposite and to the left was a family house, with housekeeper, cleaner and au-pair, mother and two young children; Dad drove an Aston Martin and was away a lot, during which time Mother had a lot of work done in the house – the place was always having something knocked down or extended. I wondered where that marriage would be in thirty years? Would he be running away with a woman half his age? I found myself getting anxious every time the kids ran out to greet Daddy when he returned home, clutching presents for the kids and flowers for the wife. I'm sure they're very happy and solid as a rock. And if not she'd probably come out of it quite well financially… lucky woman.

Fifty

Two days until I fly to Cairo. Tiptoe around the flat whispering I Believe I Can Fly. Waxed? Tick. Highlights? Tick. Tan? Tick.

I drink a pint of water, do five star jumps/squats, eat four plums, realise I've done something to my knee during jump/squats.

Zero days until I Believe I Can Fly to Cairo.

Deja vu. Once again, I am sitting in the Battered Bitch with a glass of wine in my hand. No parking tickets on the passenger seat this time; just documents and a printout from We Buy Any Car. I fondly pat the steering wheel.

"We've been through a lot together haven't we? You were there for me. Well, most of the time anyway. It's not you. It's me. I just can't afford to keep you. The repairs. The parking permits."

I jump, slopping wine over myself, when the man with the tow truck knocks on the window.

"Mrs. Watkins?"

I get out of the car. He takes in the now empty glass of wine in my hand, the look of trauma on my face.

"Saying goodbye?" he asks, surprisingly gentle for a man with that many piercings in his face. How does he get through airport security, I wonder?

"Yes. She's been there for me through thick and thin. I feel like…"

"You're betraying her?" he ends my sentence for me. I nod.

"Don't worry, love. Try and think of it more like an organ donor. She's going to help a lot of cars live healthier lives."

I blink back a rogue tear. "Thanks," I mumble, handing him the keys. "I won't watch, if that's okay?"

I sign a document and walk away from the clanking chains and whirring machinery as BB is dragged onto the back of the tow-truck.

"Fucks sake! Hurry up!" I'd asked Nicky to flat-sit for me. She was hanging out of my living room window, yelling. No wonder I couldn't make friends with anyone in this street. I only had to give her the washing machine instructions and then I was off. Off to the airport. Off to Cairo. Off to see YM who would hopefully take OFF my clothes and have it OFF with me.

Fifty-One

Arriving at Cairo airport was a magical moment. The smells, the noise, the language, hit me as I step off the plane. So wonderfully exotic. It's ten o'clock at night, the air is cool and there are no flies!

A driver is waiting for me in Arrivals and whisks me to the hotel, where YM is waiting for me in the lobby of The Kemplinski Hotel on the Corniche. He was accompanied by the tallest Nubian I have ever seen, wearing the tallest black hat I have ever seen (the Nubian was wearing the hat, not Yorkshireman). YM looked pretty gorgeous too. I hadn't imagined it; I hadn't let my imagination get the better of me. Sad face. Lovely smile.

After dropping my suitcase off in the room, we went to the rooftop bar and, with drinks in hand and pianist playing in the background, I looked out over the Nile, over the rooftops and minarets. I watched life teeming along the streets below, the smell of street food and spices wafting upwards. I could see into the British Embassy car park and pointed out to YM where the swimming pool was, where we used to collect our wine and park our car. Not the most fascinating start to YM's 'unknown Cairo tour' but I was excited to see that not much had changed in the ten years since I'd been there.

We ended up in bed that night, of course, but it was different. Nothing of the 'let's get this over with' we had had before. We talked, made love again and fell asleep in each-other's arms.

The next morning, we took a cab to Khan el-Khalili in the bazaar district – one of the most beautiful and fascinating places in the world (in my opinion). I showed YM all the gates – Bab al-Badistan and Bab al-Ghuri; the chandelier and lantern shops. We walked down Souq street and stopped off at a jewellery shop where Alli, the owner, remembered me. He treated us to a Coca-Cola while I helped YM pick out bracelets for his daughter and daughter-in-law, Ali asked where my 'first' husband was. In my pigeon Arabic I explained that William was "Dead".

In a philosophical way, he was dead and in fairness to me it was the only word I could recall in Arabic to describe the situation. I reminded myself that William brought his 'soul mate' here the day after he dumped me. So, yes, he was bloody 'dead'.

After purchasing the jewellery at Ali's and bargaining with stallholders, I took YM to a tea shop where we enjoyed a hookah pipe and mint tea in a beautiful garden near the church in Coptic Cairo. Then I showed him where I used to live and where I shopped. We walked for miles and everywhere we visited there were friendly people. I started to notice there were fewer cars and absolutely no beggars on the streets. When I lived there you couldn't go far without handing over a few coins. Maybe the increase in police numbers had something to do with it. There were certainly enough of them around now.

After a siesta (there wasn't much sleeping to be honest) we had dinner in the hotel and then went to the rooftop bar. Exhausted from our long walks (and shagging) we went to bed quite early.

The next morning, when we were in bed merrily bonking away, I felt the earth move. No, really. It moved. Not in a sexual way but literally. A kind of deep vibration.

"Somethings afoot outside," YM said.

We looked out of our window and saw the streets busy with men, young and old shouting, chanting and waving banners. We were due to leave for the airport in a few hours, but with the crowds outside growing in number and passions running high, we decided to head to the airport sooner, rather than later.

We quickly packed and, an hour later, were checked out and in a taxi, heading to the airport. The driver took the back streets out of Cairo, and even these narrow streets were full of men heading towards Tahrir Square. YM asked the driver what was happening.

"REVOLUTION!" he exclaimed. Too right, I thought, as he explained to YM the pros and cons of the Egyptian government.

To be honest I didn't take much of it in. I was sad that this wonderful country was in turmoil and little did we know that a few days later the Arab Spring would be in full flow and Cairo was now virtually a no-go area.

I was relieved when we got to the airport; it had taken a good two hours to get there and not the expected one hour. There was a sense of urgency amongst the departing passengers and airport staff, as if something significant was brewing and, as exciting as that was, I didn't fancy getting stuck in the middle of it.

When we boarded the flight YM turned left and I turned right, much to the confusion of the stewardesses. His ticket was paid for by his company, hence Business Class. He's paid for my ticket, hence Economy. I was perfectly happy about this but the stewardess, not so much. They'd decided that I was the wife of 'a tight git' and they were going to have some fun with said 'tight git'.

Once the plane had taken off and the seatbelt signs were switched off, a stewardess handed me the magazine with luxurious and unnecessary things to buy in flight; she helpfully pointed out the most expensive items. I circled a couple of things, just to be helpful. The stewardess then took the booklet to YM in Business Class.

"Credit card please, sir." YM looked concerned, unaware of any extra costs. "These have been ordered by your wife…*in Economy.*"

The stewardess returned with my Dior Essence and Magic Lash Extension mascara (see? It's not like I broke the bank).

I tried to tell him, when we landed, that it wasn't me, it was the Stewardess. YM said he was impressed by my 'brass neck'. But he didn't mind, not really. It's not as if I'd spent ten thousand pounds on a Banksy.

We walked through customs together and out into the Arrivals hall. Jenny was there to meet me, looking like an anxious parent at the school gates.

Saying goodbye to YM in front of her was very difficult; YM and I exchanged a (very) brief kiss and, before linking arms with Jenny, I watched him saunter off to catch his train and felt an immediate tug of longing. It must have been apparent because Jenny said

"Don't worry, Ma. From the way you looked at each other I'd say you'll be seeing him pretty soon."

I hoped so.